About the Sponsor

Grantmakers for Effective Organizations is a national movement of grantmakers dedicated to building strong and effective nonprofit organizations. Through research and conferences and its Web site, publications, and other activities, GEO highlights knowledge and practices in the field that advance the organizational effectiveness movement. You can reach GEO at

Grantmakers for Effective Organizations
1528 18th Street, NW
Washington, D.C. 20036
Voice: 202-518-7251
Fax: 202-518-7253
URL: www.geofunders.org
E-mail: *info@geofunders.org*

More information on GEO and a host of resources and links for funders are available at *www.geofunders.org*.

GRANTMAKERS
for EFFECTIVE
ORGANIZATIONS

Funding Effectiveness

Grantmakers for Effective Organizations
Barbara D. Kibbe
Kathleen P. Enright
Janine E. Lee
Alexa Cortes Culwell
Lisa Sobrato Sonsini
Sterling K. Speirn
Melinda T. Tuan

Funding Effectiveness

Lessons in Building Nonprofit Capacity

JOSSEY-BASS
A Wiley Imprint
www.josseybass.com

GRANTMAKERS
for EFFECTIVE
ORGANIZATIONS

Published by Jossey-Bass
A Wiley Imprint
989 Market Street, San Francisco, CA 94103-1741   www.josseybass.com

Jossey-Bass books and products are available through most bookstores. To contact Jossey-Bass directly call our Customer Care Department within the U.S. at 800-956-7739, outside the U.S. at 317-572-3986, or fax 317-572-4002.

Jossey-Bass also publishes its books in a variety of electronic formats. Some content that appears in print may not be available in electronic books.

Library of Congress Cataloging-in-Publication Data

Funding effectiveness : lessons in building nonprofit capacity / by
Grantmakers for Effective Organizations ; Barbara D. Kibbe ... [et al.].—1st ed.
  p. cm.
Includes bibliographical references and index.
  ISBN 0-7879-6816-1 (alk. paper)
  1. Nonprofit organizations—Evaluation. 2. Nonprofit
organizations—Finance. 3. Organizational effectiveness—Evaluation—Methodology.
4. Nonprofit organizations—United States. I. Kibbe, Barbara. II. Grantmakers for Effective
Organizations (Organization)
  HD2769.15.F86 2004
  658.4'01—dc22

                                                    2003020017

Printed in the United States of America
FIRST EDITION
HB Printing   10 9 8 7 6 5 4 3 2 1

Contents

Preface

Serving as GEO board chair in 2002 and 2003, I was able to witness firsthand the increasing number of funders who link an organization's capacity with its results—whether in clients served, neighborhoods brought back to life, or natural areas protected for all to enjoy. The funders that make up Grantmakers for Effective Organizations—through the activities they support and the knowledge they share—explore many possible ways to strengthen nonprofit performance. The chapters in this book highlight just a few of the successful approaches funders have used.

This book provides a rich and broad set of perspectives. It is not a book on organizational theory. Rather, it is a book that documents the approaches used by dedicated funders with years of experience.

- Barbara D. Kibbe makes the case for funding organizational effectiveness and capacity building and reflects on her years with The David and Lucile Packard Foundation.
- GEO's executive director, Kathleen P. Enright, describes the many approaches funders can take when working to improve effectiveness, using diverse examples from GEO's membership.
- Janine E. Lee, vice president, Youth Development Division, at the Ewing Marion Kauffman Foundation and current chair of GEO's board, describes the need to set clear goals and expectations when working to improve effectiveness and illustrates the impact this had on several of Kauffman's grantees.
- Alexa Cortes Culwell, CEO of the Charles and Helen Schwab Foundation, Lisa Sobrato Sonsini, founding president

of the Sobrato Family Foundation, and Sterling K. Speirn, president of the Peninsula Community Foundation, demonstrate the impact of collaboration as they tell the story of the Organizational Capacity Grants Initiative.

• Melinda T. Tuan, co-founder of The Roberts Enterprise Development Fund, emphasizes the importance of creating a culture of measurement when working to improve effectiveness.

In these chapters, the authors share their successes, explore their failures, and capture the lessons they learned along the way so that other funders will learn from these experiences. And in the Afterword, Rick Cohen of the National Committee for Responsive Philanthropy frames the authors' experiences in a broader context—the whole nonprofit and philanthropic sector, where understanding of organizational effectiveness issues may be a mile wide and an inch deep.

Nonprofit leaders can benefit from this book as well. Its contents describe the struggles funders go through to find effective ways to enhance nonprofit performance. The examples in this book show what can happen when grantmakers and grantees work together to build honest and rich relationships with one another.

Although funding effectiveness evokes much energy and passion, the field is still young, and everyone in it has much more to learn. As you read this book, I hope you will see ways to build on these lessons and experiences in your own work. And as you continue to discover new ways that funders can improve nonprofit effectiveness, I hope you will share what you learn with your colleagues—whether through GEO, a regional association of grantmakers, or other means. Thank you to all who have contributed to this expanding field through practice, research, knowledge dissemination, or funding. GEO will ensure that the learning and sharing continues.

San Francisco, California   James E. Canales
November 2003   President & CEO
                              The James Irvine Foundation

About the Authors

Rick Cohen is executive director of the National Committee for Responsive Philanthropy, the leading advocate for institutional philanthropy to provide increased access and resources to disadvantaged populations including low-income groups, racial and ethnic groups, and segments of the population facing discrimination. Before joining that organization in 1999, Cohen worked in the national office of the Local Initiatives Support Corporation as vice president of strategic planning, and before that, he was vice president of the Enterprise Foundation, where he was in charge of field services. Cohen has also worked as a private consultant and served as director of the Jersey City Department of Housing and Economic Development. Among his teaching experiences are adjunct faculty positions at Rutgers University in New Brunswick, St. Peter's College, and Columbia University. Cohen is author or coauthor of two books and many journal articles and monographs. In 2002, he was named to the "NPT Power and Influence 50," the *Nonprofit Times*'s list of the fifty most influential people in the U.S. nonprofit sector. Cohen received a bachelor of arts degree in political science from Boston University and a master's degree in city planning from the University of Pennsylvania.

Alexa Cortes Culwell is chief executive officer of the Charles and Helen Schwab Foundation, whose work is focused in two primary program areas, learning differences and human services.

Since 1992, the foundation has grown under Culwell's leadership to become nationally recognized for its work helping children with learning differences succeed in learning and life. In human services, the foundation's programs address the intersecting issues of homelessness, substance abuse, and poverty by creating model initiatives in the Bay Area that are informed by best practices nationally.

Culwell is a member of the board of directors of the Center for Effective Philanthropy, which is dedicated to improving overall foundation performance. Locally, she serves as a trustee for Northern California Grantmakers and as president of the board of Golden Gate Community, Inc., a community-based organization in San Francisco that builds businesses that employ at-risk and homeless youth. She also speaks and writes to audiences around the country about the importance of foundations being accountable for positive social impact.

Kathleen P. Enright is executive director of Grantmakers for Effective Organizations. GEO is a national movement of grantmakers dedicated to building strong and effective organizations. Through research, conferences, and its Web site, publications, and other activities, GEO highlights knowledge and practices in the field that advance the organizational effectiveness movement.

Previously, Enright served as group director, marketing and communications for BoardSource (formerly the National Center for Nonprofit Boards), where she was responsible for developing and implementing an organization-wide marketing and communications strategy, building and maintaining a consistent and recognizable brand, supervising the promotion of all products and services, and building public awareness of the importance of strong nonprofit boards. Prior to joining BoardSource, she was a project manager for the National Association of Development Organizations Research Foundation, where she directed a Ford Foundation-funded project to encourage collaboration between nonprofits and local governments.

Enright is on the board of directors of Global Education Partners and the advisory board of the Center for Effective Philanthropy. She received a bachelor's degree in English from the University of Illinois at Urbana-Champaign and a master's of public administration from The George Washington University.

Barbara D. Kibbe has twenty-five years' experience in working with and for a wide range of nonprofits and grantmakers. She is coauthor of two books: *Succeeding with Consultants*, published by the Foundation Center, and *Grantmaking Basics*, published by the Council on Foundations. She was a founder of Grantmakers for Effective Organizations (GEO), a group of nearly eight hundred funders dedicated to promoting learning and encouraging dialogue among funders committed to nonprofit and grantmaker effectiveness. From 1996 through 2002, Kibbe served as director of the Organizational Effectiveness and Philanthropy Program at the David and Lucile Packard Foundation. She is a cum laude graduate of Wagner College (New York) and earned a J.D. degree from Brooklyn Law School. She was twice selected by the *Nonprofit Times* for its annual list of the fifty most powerful and influential people in the nonprofit sector.

Janine E. Lee joined the Ewing Marion Kauffman Foundation in 1990 to manage Project STAR (Students Taught Awareness and Resistance), the foundation's nationally recognized alcohol, tobacco, and other drug use prevention program. She assumed her current duties as a youth development division vice president in 1998 and is responsible for neighborhood-based investments, the Youth Advisory Board, and the creation of the Organizational Effectiveness Investment Strategy designed to strengthen and support nonprofits.

Lee holds degrees in both rehabilitation services education and rehabilitative counseling. As part of her academic experience, she produced a research paper titled "Key Attributes of Effective Nonprofits: Serving Children, Youth and Families in Kansas City's Urban Core," which now serves as a framework for the Organizational Effectiveness Investment Strategy.

In addition to her professional responsibilities, Lee is dedicated to civic duty, serving on the Urban Affairs and Urban Planning Task Force, Kansas City's 150 Sesquicentennial Steering Committee, Leadership 2000 in Kansas City, Kansas, and Kansas City Tomorrow in Kansas City, Missouri. Lee represents the Kauffman Foundation as a founder and current board chair of Grantmakers for Effective Organizations. She is also a lifetime member of the National Black MBA Association.

Lisa Sobrato Sonsini is board president of the Sobrato Family Foundation, which is dedicated to helping create and sustain a vibrant and healthy community where all Silicon Valley residents have equal opportunity to live, work, and be enriched. Sonsini focuses her volunteer time with community-based organizations helping abused and neglected youth, currently as board president of Child Advocates of Santa Clara and San Mateo Counties and board secretary of the Silicon Valley Children's Fund. She is active in promoting philanthropy among young donors, and she assisted in the formation of Silicon Valley Social Ventures (SV2). In her capacity as a grantmaker, Sonsini serves on the board of Northern California Grantmakers and the advisory board of Community Foundation Silicon Valley. She was inducted into the San Mateo County Women's Hall of Fame in 2001 and was a member of Class XIV of the American Leadership Forum, Silicon Valley. Prior to establishing the Sobrato Family Foundation in 1996, Sonsini practiced as a corporate associate at the law firm of Brobeck, Phleger and Harrison. She earned her law degree in 1991 from Boalt Hall, University of California at Berkeley.

Sterling K. Speirn is president of the Peninsula Community Foundation. In his first twelve years at the foundation, Speirn launched the Center for Venture Philanthropy, co-founded the Peninsula Partnership for Children, Youth and Families, and led PCF as it grew from $44 million to more than $470 million in total assets.

Speirn is chair of the statewide League of California Community Foundations, serves on the advisory boards of Pacific Community Ventures and the Entrepreneurs' Foundation, and is on the boards of directors of the American Leadership Forum of Silicon Valley and Northern California Grantmakers.

He holds a degree in political science from Stanford and a law degree from the University of Michigan. In 1986, he joined Apple Computer and led the company's national computer grants program for nearly four years. In 2000 and 2001 he taught a graduate seminar on philanthropy at the Stanford Graduate School of Business.

Melinda T. Tuan co-founded The Roberts Enterprise Development Fund in 1997, with Jed Emerson and George R. Roberts. Prior to her work with REDF, Tuan was a manager at a national health-care nonprofit and a management consultant specializing in growth strategies for Fortune 500 companies. Tuan has volunteered with numerous community-based organizations in Honolulu, Boston, and the San Francisco Bay Area that serve homeless and low-income populations. Additionally, she co-founded Boston Cares, a nonprofit volunteer service organization, and was involved in the start-up of a social-mission-driven company called Dayspring Technologies in San Francisco. Tuan serves on the boards of directors for Grantmakers for Effective Organizations, Evergreen Lodge (a destination lodge in Yosemite with a social mission), and the Stanford Business School Alumni Association.

Tuan graduated from Harvard University with a bachelor's degree in social studies and an emphasis on urban poverty and homelessness. She also holds an MBA and a certificate in nonprofit management from the Stanford Graduate School of Business.

Chapter One

Investing in Nonprofit Capacity

Barbara D. Kibbe

In recent years, a growing number of nonprofit leaders—representing grantmakers and grantseekers alike—have embraced the importance of investing in the capacity and effectiveness of individual organizations and of the sector as a whole. The signs of change are both profound and plentiful:

- The *Chronicle on Philanthropy* and *Foundation News and Commentary* now regularly feature articles on organizational effectiveness, capacity building, and related topics.
- Nearly 150 colleges and universities around the country offer graduate courses in nonprofit management—up from only 32 in the early 1990s.
- Researchers are devoting increased attention to issues of nonprofit organizational effectiveness, producing new data on what makes organizations work and how to make them stronger.
- The literature on nonprofit leadership, management, and governance expands constantly. Jossey-Bass—the publisher of this volume—now adds dozens of new titles per year to the total, and it is far from the only source of advice and insight.
- Founded in 1997, Grantmakers for Effective Organizations (GEO) boasts nearly eight hundred members from nearly six hundred grantmaking organizations. GEO is creating knowledge and building community to enhance dialogue and improve practice in the field.

Perhaps the most important indication of how the nonprofit sector is embracing the need to build organizational capacity and effectiveness is the way funders throughout the country are incorporating this perspective into their grantmaking work. Foundation Center statistics show a marked increase in funding for organizational effectiveness in recent years. Grants for capacity building grew from $300 million to $400 million in a single year (1998 to 1999); technical assistance grants alone rose by a remarkable 180 percent during the 1990s (Light, 2002). In 2002, research by Tom Backer of the Human Interaction Research Institute identified more than 350 funder-based organizational capacity-building programs in the United States.

Instead of focusing exclusively on funding programs and individual projects, this strong and growing community of grantmakers is taking a harder look at what makes grantee programs and projects succeed or fail. They are investing in building strong organizations to house effective programs. Although capacity is not the same as effectiveness, funders are becoming increasingly convinced that strong management, leadership, and governance are linked to overall effectiveness and impact.

Today, targeted capacity-building support is as varied as the funders themselves in terms of focus and as broad as the needs of the nonprofits they serve. Capacity-building efforts range from help with technology or facilities to organizational assessment, planning, leadership development, and evaluation.

Despite all the attention to organizational capacity building and its potential to propel the nonprofit sector to higher levels of performance in the years ahead, no widely accepted definition of either nonprofit organizational effectiveness or nonprofit capacity currently exists. Not surprisingly, there remains a lack of understanding and consensus about how funders can best build the capacity and effectiveness of grantees. To state it more succinctly, we simply don't know enough about what works best under which circumstances.

Defining Effectiveness

Developing practical, useful, robust definitions of *capacity* and *effectiveness* is difficult but critical to building needed knowledge so that capacity-building resources can focus on what works. Anyone who works with nonprofits can describe organizations that are marvelously effective but may not manage every aspect of their organization according to the textbook—along with many efficient organizations that fall short when it comes to results. An organization, like an organism, is dynamic. The health and effectiveness of an organization require constant attention and upkeep. To reduce organizational effectiveness to a checklist is to deny the inherent complexity of organizational life.

This highlights one of the dangers in defining terms—the easy way out is to equate efficiency and effectiveness because efficiency is easier to describe, but capacity is not an end in itself. Capacities that enhance effectiveness (or results) are capacities that are aligned with and in service of mission and goals.

Another complicating factor is trying to determine whose perspective is most important in assessing an organization's effectiveness. *Effectiveness* is a relative term. Over the years, researchers have documented real and continuing shifts in thinking about effectiveness (Forbes, 1998; Herman and Renz, 1999).

Three decades ago, it was generally accepted that an effective organization was one that attained its goals, but what if an organization sets goals that are modest and easily attainable? What if an organization achieves its goals but does so at a cost much greater than others doing similar work? Does that mean that the resources under its direction are insufficiently leveraged? A competing view equates effectiveness with sustainability—if an organization can keep itself going, it's successful. Yet another view is that effectiveness is in the eyes of the beholder—that an organization's constituents should determine its effectiveness. But different constituents can and often do have inconsistent—or even opposing—views of an organization.

Whose opinion counts most—the client? the donor? the board of directors? the regulatory agency that oversees the field? the media?

GEO has created an aspirational definition of *organizational effectiveness:* "the ability of an organization to fulfill its mission by measurably achieving its objectives through a blend of sound management, strong governance, and a persistent rededication to assessing and achieving results." Both program design and measurement of results in the capacity-building field would advance quickly if leaders agreed on a basic set of definitions, aligned their programs and goals with those definitions, and committed to evaluating their progress at achieving greater non-profit capacity through their grantmaking. As a conversation starter, I offer the following working definitions—built from the ideas of many thoughtful capacity builders and funders of capacity building.

Organizational effectiveness is the ability of an organization to define a meaningful mission, generate the tangible and intangible resources required to advance that mission, and deploy those resources efficiently and well in the accomplishment of its work. Four organizational capacities significantly contribute to and sustain organizational effectiveness over time:

- *Technical capacity* to define, deliver, and evaluate programs consistent with promising practices in the field
- *Management capacity* to align policies, processes, and resources with desired outcomes
- *Resource development capacity* to assemble adequate physical and human resources as well as a diverse, reliable, and sustainable flow of financial assets
- *Leadership capacity* to build support among varied constituencies, participate in social and policy dialogue, and govern the organization in such a way as to continuously renew its position in a changing context

Organizational capacity building is the application of knowledge and expertise to the enhancement of those factors that contribute to organizational effectiveness. Capacity building focuses on an organization's skills, systems, structures, and strategies. The primary intent of organizational capacity building is to enhance an organization's ability to achieve its social mission.

In an attempt to strengthen these definitions so they can be widely used by the field, GEO welcomes the feedback of thinkers and practitioners in the field.

Until researchers and the field develop these definitions and forge consensus, some funders are independently defining *capacity* for their own purposes. In Chapter Three, Janine E. Lee describes the research she conducted to create a list of attributes of effective organizations to help guide the Ewing Marion Kauffman Foundation's work. Granted, this independent approach involves some risks: grantees can be buffeted by conflicting advice, and grantmakers focused on building nonprofit capacity find it difficult to measure outcomes for their work or to learn from each other because core assumptions are often so different. Regardless, it is critical to have *some* way to define the work, or grantmaking efforts will lack direction, and their impact will be difficult to demonstrate.

The Building Blocks of Capacity

In this less-than-perfect world, populated by complex organizations with multiple goals and varying capabilities, some comfort can be taken in one simple truth and its corollary:

- *The truth:* Many types of capacity and many different competencies are useful or essential to helping a nonprofit organization achieve its goals.
- *The corollary:* Different organizations, working in different fields, will require different capacities at different times and at different stages of development.

An arts organization, for example, may need a strong marketing capability to attract an audience for its programs. A community development corporation, on the other hand, may have a greater need for legal and political expertise to advance its plans for neighborhood revitalization.

According to many thought leaders and practitioners in the field of nonprofit capacity building, three central aspects of organizational capacity are essential to all (or nearly all) successful nonprofit organizations:

- Planfulness
- Effective leadership
- Strong governance

Of course, nonprofits need not excel in every area to be effective, but they do need certain key capacities to be strong and successful. Strong governance, effective leadership, and what we call "planfulness" are crucial, and funders can play an important role in developing these capacities. For the relationship between capacity-building funders and grantees to succeed, and to result in improved capacity for nonprofits, funders would be well advised to pay attention to their own capabilities as well—building their own capacity to diagnose organizational challenges and aligning their policies and practices with the outcomes they hope to achieve and the capacities they hope to build.

Planfulness

Nonprofit organizations by their very nature struggle to get the maximum leverage out of limited resources. This means developing a clear-cut mission, ambitious but achievable goals, measurable objectives, sustainable strategies, and disciplined implementation aligned with known best practices in any given field.

A planful organization is thoughtful about its mission and direction. It maximizes the use of its resources to approach opportunities and challenges. It is aware of its own capabilities and limitations in an ever-changing world.

Planfulness is the capacity to revisit the organization's mission, goals, and strategies on a regular basis to make sure they are fresh and appropriate to new opportunities, new challenges, and changes in the wider world. The kind of planfulness that is a hallmark of a highly effective nonprofit is not merely an activity and is much more than a one-time strategic planning project. It is a set of skills, a process, an orientation, and a commitment.

Expert facilitation and consultation can have a profound effect on helping nonprofits to build relevant and powerful plans and— even more important—helping to engender the attitude and practice of planfulness in an organization. The role of funders in encouraging and supporting planfulness in grantees is an obvious one. Financial support for a planning consultant or the costs associated with a planning process can transform an organization that lurches from one crisis to another into a resilient team of people with a common understanding of the goals and challenges ahead and how to address them.

Effective Leadership

Planfulness is an important skill for effective leadership, but a leader must do much more than plan. Effective leaders have a vision, articulate that vision in a compelling way, and engage others so they feel a personal stake in an organization's success. Effective leaders model the behavior they wish to see in others throughout their organization and embody the organizational culture.

Effective nonprofit leaders are equal parts politician, cheerleader, change agent, and manager. They are capable of marshaling an organization's people and its resources for maximum effect. In addition, it is the leader's job to look outward and to build alliances with other organizations. More than anyone else, the leader is responsible for the tone and substance of the organization's interactions with funders, the media, clients, and other constituencies.

While leaders cannot be expected to excel at all these roles simultaneously, funders can help them develop and nurture the necessary skills and competencies through support for coaching, training, and peer-to-peer learning.

Strong Governance

It is a fact of life for nonprofits as well as for-profits that a well-governed organization is more likely than a poorly governed one to achieve its goals. When a board is unprepared to fulfill its role, when its members are disengaged or embroiled in conflict with each other or with the staff, even an organization with a sound plan, good management, and an inspired and committed leader can fail.

The exemplary nonprofit board functions as an essential resource for its organization—a source of knowledge, expertise, vision, resources, and contacts in the community. Board members should understand their legal responsibilities and be committed to fulfilling their role with energy and integrity. By developing its board, a nonprofit organization can go a long way toward improving its overall effectiveness as well as its capacity to carry out its plans. Yet nonprofit boards rarely see their own development as a priority. Here again, a funder's encouragement and modest resources can yield extraordinary results. Support for training a board to undertake a major donor campaign can help reduce stress and ensure the success of a critical board-staff joint project. Support for an executive director and board chair to attend a workshop together can build skills and cement their relationship, which is the most critical working relationship in any organization.

The nonprofit's path to effectiveness can to a great degree be defined as appropriate attention to leadership, governance, and planning. What then is the funder's role in building these core capacities or other important specific capabilities? How can a grant-maker ensure that the support offered is itself effective?

Capacity Building: What It Takes from Funders

Nonprofit organizations, together with the communities they serve, can reap huge rewards when funders provide resources, knowledge, and skill-building opportunities aimed at increasing effectiveness. Simply stated, both grantmaker and grantee are much better off if both parties pay close attention to the overall organizational strengths and challenges facing the grantee.

Funders who are committed to improving their own effectiveness tend to have greater credibility in working with nonprofits. When funders pay attention to their own capacities—when they "walk the talk"—they are seen by grantees as sincere and trusted partners. The journey to effectiveness can be one that nonprofits and their funders take together, learning from each other and sharing with each other along the way.

When working in partnership with nonprofits to build capacity, funders should pay attention to their own capacities in four areas: knowledge, flexibility, humility, and commitment.

Knowledge

We define *knowledge* as "familiarity, awareness, or an understanding gained through experience or study." The term can also refer to learning and erudition.

Grantmaking focused on building organizational capacity and effectiveness is not something a funder can or should undertake on a whim. To contribute in a positive way to an organization's effectiveness, capacity-building efforts should be based on a solid understanding of organizational theory and practice. Even small nonprofit organizations are complex systems. Funders, to put it bluntly, need to know what they are doing, because a naive approach can do real harm. Funders can unwittingly confuse grantees with casual observations or misdirect a grantee with advice that is off the mark. Imagine the dangers of a situation where a single nonprofit has multiple funders, all of which put a high priority on building capacity and effectiveness but each of which favors a different path to enlightenment.

The risk of mandating capacity-building work, if defined by a funder who lacks knowledge of this complex and rapidly evolving field, is that grantees may be compelled to focus on the wrong area or to invest precious time and resources in something trivial in their own context simply because it has been seen as important elsewhere. Of course, it is people who hold and build knowledge. Whether they are brought in as consultants or hired as full-time foundation staff, the people who are making capacity-building grants can be effective only to the extent that they have relevant training and experience that enable them to diagnose organizational issues and intervene sensitively to help organizations build skills and reflect on systems, strategies, and structures.

The funder is not the only knowledgeable person in this complex equation. The grantee's members will know their organization better than any funder ever will. That deep experience should be acknowledged and respected. In the right balance, the grantee's deep knowledge and the funder's perspective should combine to catalyze insight for positive learning and change.

Few funders directly provide the capacity-building services needed by nonprofits, so funders need not become experts in all aspects of organizational development. More commonly, the funder considers the grantee's needs, coaches gently, brokers resources, and funds a grantee's efforts. In these cases, the funder and the grantee often come to rely on the expertise and experience of an independent third party—a consultant, trainer, or coach.

Selecting the right consultant for a given project can be key to a successful outcome. The right consultant is someone with a rich variety of experience, including experience in the field in which the grantee works. Such consultants have seen how different issues can appear in different organizations. They have developed a relevant and reasonably comprehensive toolkit of approaches and strategies for helping an organization succeed. Great dividends are realized when a consultant is committed to skills transfer, leaving behind new competencies as a result of the consulting engagement.

There is no shortcut to knowledge. The most expeditious way for a funder to acquire deep expertise in organizational development and management is to hire someone who already possesses the invaluable experience of actually having run a nonprofit organization. For smaller funders, this may mean working with respected consultants and experts or working through trusted intermediaries, but it is also of great value to train program staff in the basics of organizational diagnosis.

Staying Current. Just as essential as a practical and tested understanding of organizational development and capacity building is a familiarity with the current literature on organizational effectiveness. Part of the expectation for foundation staff and consultants working on these issues should be that they are up to date. New information on nonprofit performance and effectiveness is appearing all the time. Awareness of the latest findings and familiarity with the practices (and results) of other grantmakers are among the best ways to ensure that limited capacity-building dollars are deployed for the greatest effect. To assist in this effort, Grantmakers for Effective Organizations provides a comprehensive and frequently updated list of tools and resources relevant to the capacity-building grantmaker on its Web site, www.geofunders.org.

Reflection Is a Virtue. It is not just *outside* sources of knowledge and information that contribute to the success of capacity-building efforts. Often, grantmakers forget all the *inside* sources of information they have access to—including qualitative and quantitative data on the results of current and past capacity-building efforts undertaken with their own grantees.

Ideally, a commitment to helping build the organizational effectiveness of nonprofits should be paralleled by a funder's own internal commitment to continuous learning and improvement. Funders of capacity-building and organizational effectiveness can contribute importantly to building knowledge so the field can continue to advance.

One low-cost, high-yield approach to building knowledge based on experience is to take time to reflect on completed capacity-building grants. A review of the original proposal file and reports, combined with a brief telephone interview with the grantee, can help to draw out lessons for future grantmaking. You may want to ask your grantees questions like these:

- What unexpected challenges did you face in connection with your capacity-building efforts? How did you address these challenges?

- What key lessons were learned through the process? How are these lessons being put into practice?

- What difference did this effort make in the overall effectiveness of your program or organization?

- How would you approach this project if you were to start over, knowing what you know now?

- What advice would you give to other organizations about to embark on a similar effort?

- How could we (as your funder) improve our approach in the future?

Making this kind of commitment to reflect on each capacity-building grant at its close (or shortly thereafter) has several benefits. It will give you a better sense of the challenges facing grantees in their efforts to enhance organizational effectiveness and an improved ability to connect the capacity-building effort to its purpose—improved effectiveness in pursuit of mission and goals. This input, in turn, can lead to improved processes and guidelines for better customer service, as well as better alignment of process with hoped-for outcomes and, ultimately, greater impact of the funder's capacity-building efforts.

Questions for Funders

- Do we have (or have access to) expertise in the areas of organizational development and nonprofit management?

- Are there ways in which we operate that impede rather than bolster grantee effectiveness? (For example, are our proposal or reporting guidelines overly burdensome? Is our decision-making process so cumbersome that it takes several months for us to act on a capacity-building grant?)

- Are we committed to keeping up to date on research in the fields of nonprofit management and organizational effectiveness and capacity building?

- Are we staffed adequately and appropriately to enable us to add value to the capacity-building work of our grantees?

- Do we adequately reflect on the outcomes of our capacity-building grantmaking? Are we continually improving on our approach based on current research?

- Can we invest in external evaluation so that we contribute to building knowledge for ourselves and for the field?

- Are we learning? And are we using what we are learning?

Flexibility

We define *flexibility* as "a ready capability to adapt to new, different, or changing requirements." The term also describes responsiveness to change and adaptability.

Of course, an in-depth knowledge of organizational development and capacity building should be coupled with the understanding that every organization is different and that even the same organization will have different capacity-building challenges at different times. Although the rich array of assessment tools and checklists can help in diagnosing organizational needs and challenges, these tools are most helpful if seen as guides for discussion and inquiry rather than as report cards. Organizations do not exist in a laboratory environment. The most effective funders of capacity building create thoughtful and appropriately flexible systems for providing support.

If, for example, a valued grantee experiences an unexpected executive transition at a time when the only capacity-building support available is for planning, it faces an important misalignment between resources and needs, and the greatest capacity-building opportunity—to help the grantee organization recruit or train the right new leader—will be missed.

Flexibility means more than the ability to redirect funds when the situation warrants. It also means respecting a grantee's own expertise and perspective as it shapes and administers its programs and its organization. As long as the grantee's capacity-building priorities are arrived at thoughtfully and are in line with its mission, a funder should be circumspect in dispensing advice or redirecting the effort and slow to criticize. This is not to say that the objectivity of a third-party expert is not useful; in many cases it is critical. But the funder is rarely able to be both fully informed about a grantee's organizational challenges and entirely objective. Engaging a consultant can help a grantee reflect on the difficult issues in a safe environment that encourages honest inquiry.

In addition, capacity-building challenges may emerge suddenly and without warning—for example, when a major funding stream is disrupted. These are not times to abandon an organization or to retreat and wait for things to blow over. They are rather opportunities for a funder to help the organization rethink its niche, adjust its goals, reformulate its plans, or perhaps even consider merger with another organization. If the organization's mission remains one that the funder supports, why not show flexibility in supporting the organization as it figures out how to keep delivering on its mission in new and different ways?

Although flexibility is often required for successful capacity-building efforts, it does not mean going wobbly and blindly agreeing to fund anything the grantee suggests. Rather, it means avoiding the tendency to define the capacity-building project without taking the time to look objectively at the challenges the grantee is facing, along with its assets and opportunities. It means acknowledging that some of the greatest benefits of an effort to build organizational capacity are the lessons individuals learn through the process. It may also mean that ending up with a different set of assumptions (and therefore objectives) than people started with at the beginning of the process may signal the biggest success of all.

Flexibility confers other benefits on grantmakers above and beyond their role in focusing everyone's attention on the urgent issues confronting an organization. The most important ancillary benefit can be seen in the quality of the grantmaker-grantee relationship itself. Guidelines and reporting requirements that are unnecessarily rigid can actually lead to a lack of candor on the part of the grantee, who may feel compelled to spend time and energy trying to figure out what the funder wants instead of focusing on the real needs of the organization. Working together to identify and address management, leadership, and governance challenges—a simple fact of life for every organization—can and often does lead to more authentic grantmaker-grantee relationships.

Simply stated, any funder who shows more interest in what the grantee is learning than in whether the work plan is being followed exactly as laid out will be building a more authentic relationship with the grantee.

Questions for Funders

- Do our guidelines allow us to support grantees in addressing a fairly wide range of common capacity and effectiveness issues?

- Are we able to be flexible about deadlines and reporting requirements as long as the grantee is learning and progressing through the capacity-building process?

- Do our grantees see us as partners in the capacity-building process? Do they know what kind of reporting and accountability is required?

- Have we looked at trends in the organizational capacity issues that grantees are facing and adjusted our programs to better serve their emerging needs?

Humility

We define *humility* as "meekness or modesty in behavior, attitude or spirit." The term also indicates freedom from arrogance and pride, as well as the ability to show deference.

Humility is closely related to the notion of flexibility. Holding on to your humility when you occupy a grantmaker's chair can take real effort. The primary reason for grantmakers to remind themselves to remain humble in their relationships with grantees is that there is a real power differential at work. Even a gentle suggestion from a grantmaker will often be heard as a directive, and it is all too easy to misdirect an organization with a careless remark.

In recent years, the venture capital model of philanthropy, where the funder is providing much more than financial support and may even take on a role in governing or managing the grantee organization, has been tested and much debated. The conversation about its relevance to the work of all types of grantmakers has been edifying and rich. At the same time, grantmakers should remember that true venture capitalists get feedback that is tangible and immediate. If they give good advice along with their investment capital, they often make money, placing them in a position to make more investments and give more good advice. In philanthropy, it is not so clear when a grantmaker's advice is constructive. Funders can continue to make grants indefinitely; the real risk is borne by the grantee. Grantees may feel compelled to act on the advice of funders, whether that advice is good or bad. It is the rare grantee who will return to a funder with honest feedback. Whether the risk is real or imagined, telling a funder the truth often seems too dangerous to attempt.

The key point here is that successful capacity building requires a commitment to the principle that learning and change should be driven in large part by nonprofits themselves; a funder operating at a distance will rarely know enough to prescribe just the right approach. Similarly, even the right approach will fail without substantial commitment from the organization's leadership—commitment that comes from thinking through the problem and arriving at a proposed solution independently rather than having one imposed from outside.

The more decisions grantees make for themselves, the more committed they are to the process and the project. For example, coaching a grantee on how to select a consultant is more beneficial than choosing the consultant the granter regards as best for the grantee. Not only does this ensure a better fit between the organization and the consultant; the consultant search and selection process itself becomes a learning experience as the organization grapples with the question of what it needs.

Of course, grantmakers have every right to insist on thoughtfulness as grantees develop and implement capacity-building projects— but they should avoid the impulse to dictate what or how grantees think.

Questions for Funders

- Are our guidelines really guiding our grantees? Do they adequately describe our hoped-for outcomes in funding capacity building so that grantees are able to understand our values and approach?

- Are we clear about our expectations and hoped-for outcomes of grantees' capacity-building projects? Are these outcomes negotiated with the grantees?

- Are we actively seeking feedback from grantees in order to improve our approach?

- Are we open to hearing about and learning from a failed capacity-building effort?

- Are we accessible to our grantees during the proposal process?

- Are we willing to share the issues we are struggling with as a funder and admit when we've made a mistake?

Commitment

We define a *commitment* as an "obligation or pledge."

A major criticism leveled at funders is lack of staying power—priorities seem to change at times and in ways that are often confusing to grantees. If it is true that change is constant, then a grantmaker's capacity-building work requires unflagging attention. There is no quick fix—and no permanent fix either—as nonprofit organizations confront an ever-changing context for their work. To stay relevant and continue to serve their clients and communities effectively, nonprofits must regularly reinvent themselves and refresh their missions. Frequently, one capacity-building initiative will uncover another capacity-building need. Planning may uncover a need for restructuring. A fundraising feasibility study may uncover the need to focus on training for the board. Funders of capacity building must commit themselves to making it a priority for the long term.

In fact, renewed and even increased commitment to organizational capacity building in times of organizational change can pay big dividends. Since the success of a funder is almost entirely dependent on the success of its grantees, the most constructive view of grantees' capacity-building challenges is to see them as opportunities to help grantees rethink, reposition, and reengineer.

For example, some might say it is counterintuitive to rush in with extra funds when an organization loses an executive director. A funder could be seen as prudent for wanting to wait and see who will be steering the organization before committing to or renewing a grant, but if the funder is truly committed to the organization and its mission, why not make a grant to help ensure that the search process for the executive director is thoughtful and thorough? Executive transition is one of the most challenging situations any organization will face. It is also one of the most crucial to the organization's future success. Boards are often inclined to hurry through the selection process for fear an extended period of transition will be devastating. Funders can show support in a number of ways:

- Provide funding for a search firm to ensure a rigorous selection process.
- Provide funding to hire an interim executive director.
- Let the board know that the funder understands the importance of the decision and that finding the right person may take time.

Capacity building is never easy. It takes more time and more effort than anyone thinks. For a funder, the difficulty of this work—even if it is more than made up for by the potential rewards—underscores the importance of a top-down commitment to doing it right. If capacity building is merely a peripheral concern for selected staff, the impact will be limited. The funder's leadership needs to embrace it as a priority and devote the necessary time and resources to make a real difference in improving the effectiveness of grantees.

Commitment to organizational effectiveness, of course, goes both ways. The grantee must have a sincere commitment to the effort; the commitment of the funder alone will not suffice. The presence of an internal champion for the work will increase the chances of success. Grantees have important, often urgent work to do. Without someone beating the drum for capacity building from inside, this work can easily be left on the back burner in favor of other, more directly program-related priorities. Capacity building is an ongoing, never-ending effort, and funders can come in at various points along the way to provide support. True commitment to organizational effectiveness is evidenced in every decision an organization makes and the way in which it relates to the world around it.

Questions for Funders

- Are we able to stay with our grantees over the long term?
- Is the commitment to capacity building embraced by our trustees and executive leadership?
- Are the resources allocated to capacity building adequate to achieve the hoped-for outcomes?
- Is the approach to capacity building well aligned—and integrated—with our overall grantmaking programs and priorities?

Exemplary Capacity Builders

Strengthening nonprofit effectiveness is a journey undertaken by funders and their nonprofit partners. And funders often make use of external resources to deliver capacity-building support and services to their grantees. Needless to say, these resources—people and organizations—vary in their skill levels and ability to catalyze positive change for an organization. The most exemplary capacity-builders exhibit the following characteristics:

- A deep understanding of grantee organizations and their constituents
- Expertise and experience directly relevant to the job at hand
- Awareness of developments in the field
- Commitment to continual learning and improvement of their own skills
- Openness to feedback
- Active engagement in a community of practice
- Enthusiasm for sharing learnings and for learning from the experience of others
- Commitment to skill building for nonprofit partners
- Ability to look beyond organizational dynamics to see the whole system
- Awareness of personal limitations

Looking Inward

Embracing capacity building as a priority forces a funder to look inward—not only at its own capacity to carry out this important work but also at the overall effectiveness of its grantmaking systems. Attention to the capacity-building needs of grantees will highlight the need for more research and evaluation concerning what makes organizations effective, what types of capacity-building interventions work best in what situations, and what those interventions buy in terms of program outcomes.

Over the past ten years, investing in the capacity of organizations has moved from a sideline concern to a mainstream strategy embraced by a widening network of foundations throughout the country. Organizations such as the Omidyar Foundation and the William O'Neill Foundation, for instance, have recently embraced capacity building as a major focus of their grantmaking. Nonetheless, the base of research and "lessons learned" remains insufficient to guide the field as it moves along this path.

Although most approaches to capacity building have certain strengths and weaknesses, evaluation and information sharing can help build the knowledge that will lead funders toward strategies that work. The information and the lessons in this book are offered as a starting point and an overview for funders who want to do more to improve the effectiveness of the organizations they support.

Subsequent chapters highlight the success of a variety of funders in building planfulness, nurturing effective leadership, and encouraging strong governance in their nonprofit partners. As the stories unfold, the reader will see how, time and again, funders' knowledge, flexibility, humility, and commitment enabled them to leverage capacity-building investments into real results.

These traits reappear as themes throughout this book in the lessons that follow. In Chapter Two, GEO Executive Director Kathleen Enright makes a case for *flexibility* in grantmaking in her descriptions of various organizational effectiveness approaches. In Chapter Three, Janine Lee describes the *knowledge* the Ewing Marion Kauffman Foundation has gained from working with its nonprofit partners. The Organizational Capacity Grants Initiative (a joint effort of the Charles and Helen Schwab Foundation, the Sobrato Family Foundation and the Peninsula Community Foundation), described in Chapter Four, provides a classic example of *commitment* to building effectiveness; when the funders found their project could not be completed in two years as planned, they

Questions for Grantseekers to Consider

Grantseekers need to do some advance thought and planning of their own to be sure that the capacity-building help they accept will be likely to accomplish what they need.

- Have we adequately diagnosed our capacity-building needs so that we can describe a thoughtful process for building the capacity of our organization?

- Are we committed to the real work of organizational capacity building and willing to commit the time and energy of staff and leadership to the job?

- Is this funder respectful of our knowledge of our own organization and the challenges we face?

- Is the support offered by this funder well aligned with our organization's needs?

- Is the funder interested in learning from the experience of this grant or project?

- Do we trust the funder enough to describe what really happened, without painting an artificially rosy picture?

- Will this funder allow for a change in grant terms or objectives based on early learning if needed?

- Are we actively learning from our interactions with this funder? Can they lead us to useful information and resources to help with our capacity-building efforts?

committed a third year to their nonprofit partners. The story of *humility* that Melinda Tuan provides in Chapter Five is something funders should remember in their own work—when The Roberts Enterprise Development Fund realized the evaluation systems it was creating for its portfolio enterprises were not working out, the fund was not too proud to admit its mistakes and work with the nonprofits to create a system that worked for everyone involved.

As you read through these stories of funders at work to build the capacity of grantees, the authors all hope you can find lessons to apply to your own work. As you learn new lessons in your capacity-building work, we hope you share them with colleagues—through GEO, or your local regional association, or less formally—to help advance this evolving field.

Lessons Learned: One Grantmaker's Experience

During its seventeen-year life span, the David and Lucile Packard Foundation's Organizational Effectiveness and Philanthropy program learned many lessons for grantmakers through a process of trial and error, study and reflection, and—most important—direct feedback from grantees. Here are some of the most useful insights the program developed:

1. **Management challenges are normal and ongoing for all organizations.** Management challenges emerge not because an organization is weak or poorly run but as a result of healthy growth, risk taking, and adaptation to a rapidly changing environment. A commitment to addressing these challenges is a sign of strength, not weakness.

2. **Organizational effectiveness grantmakers should insist on thoughtfulness as grantees develop projects, not on what or how grantees should think.** There are many paths to competency and many kinds of capacity. Understandably, grantseekers will be less committed to funders' priorities than to their own. And grantseekers know their business better than funders ever will.

3. **The more decisions the grantseeker makes, the more committed it will be to the process and the project.** This makes it essential for the grantmaker to work to reduce the effects of the power differential implicit in the funding process, which can make even a gentle suggestion from a grantmaker sound like a directive.

4. **Grantmakers will get more leverage from coaching a grantee on how to select a consultant than from choosing the "best" consultant for the grantee.** The skills, experience, and quality of the consultant or other technical assistance provider have a direct impact on the outcomes for the organization, but the organization must understand and welcome what the consultant has to offer before it will really benefit from the relationship. This makes the consultant search and selection process a critical step for the organization attempting to enhance its organizational effectiveness.

5. **There is no quick fix, nor is there a permanent fix.** Effectiveness requires ongoing attention because change is the constant. Since the context for the work is always changing, the organization must change as well.

6. **Renewed, even increased commitment in times of organizational change can pay big dividends.** A funder's success is almost entirely dependent upon the success of its grantees. Both share a common vision and goal. The bumps they encounter along the way are opportunities to rethink, reposition, and reengineer. When an organization loses its executive director, a funder may be inclined to wait and see who the new executive is before renewing a grant. Nonetheless, funds aimed at helping ensure that the search process is thoughtful and thorough may be the best investment of all.

7. **It's beneficial to define the relationship and the process up front.** Honesty in reporting and authenticity in the grantmaker-grantee relationship can either be enhanced or seriously damaged in connection with this work. Trust is not a static condition. For better or worse, the power differential between funder and grantee means that maintaining productive and healthy relationships requires constant attention.

8. **An internal champion for the capacity-building work is vital to the success of the project.** Grantees have their own

chosen or assigned missions to carry out. Capacity building needs its own champion within the organization to keep it from being shoved into the background in the face of program-related priorities.

9. **Organization building takes longer and is harder than anyone thinks.** Grantees who look back on organizational effectiveness work constantly report this phenomenon. Holding an organizational effectiveness grantee to a tight timeline can actually inhibit learning and lead to posturing and lack of candor in reporting. It's much more productive to reassure grantees that the funder will extend a grant period if progress is being made and more time is needed.

10. **A grant for planning, training, assessment, or evaluation will not help an organization in crisis.** A true crisis—earthquake, fire, flood, unanticipated loss of funding, or sudden and complete breakdown in the relationship between the executive director and the board—is not the right time for a thoughtful, comprehensive process. An organizational effectiveness grant will not have the desired results when what is needed is a quick infusion of cash or immediate action to deal with an emergency. On the other hand, a crisis caused by poor governance, inadequate organizational systems or structures, misalignment between programs and mission, or any other significant organizational failing will never be effectively addressed by an infusion of cash.

11. **We still know too little about how to do grantmaking to promote organizational effectiveness or what its true impact is.** Grantmakers can contribute to the knowledge base and to the development of best practices by being thoughtful, reflecting on the work and sharing lessons learned.

Chapter Two

Flexible Frameworks for Organizational Effectiveness

Kathleen P. Enright, Executive Director, Grantmakers for Effective Organizations

While few funders would question the benefits of nonprofits' having strong infrastructures and effective operations, many may scratch their heads in wonder when asked how to define an effective organization. As difficult as it may be to understand what effectiveness is, it can be just as hard to figure out how to get there. As mentioned in Chapter One, an agreed-upon definition will certainly help funders and nonprofits alike in their pursuit of organizational effectiveness, but it will not come with a road map to follow to reach this idyllic state.

This book presents some definitions and a framework of general capacities of effective organizations. Coupled with the lessons provided from other funders, it can offer insights and guidance, but ultimately it is up to individual organizations and the funders that support them to create a description of an effective organization to strive toward and a plan for achieving that goal of effectiveness.

This work is complicated by the multitude of players working on and thinking about organizational effectiveness issues:

- *Nonprofit organizations*—that strive every day to work effectively at achieving their missions
- *Management support organizations and associations*—that work with nonprofits to provide technical assistance and support on a variety of issues

- *Researchers and academic centers*—that search for quantitative data to demonstrate common characteristics of effective organizations and the impact of strengthening a nonprofit on the sector and the community

- *National infrastructure organizations*—that help nonprofits with specific issues such as governance, communications, or technology or advocate on the sector's behalf

- *Grantmaking organizations*—that partner with nonprofits to strengthen the sector and achieve results

The progress and perspectives of these multiple players enhance what we know about the sector, but they also present challenges for collective learning and improvement. All of us working on this issue have the same ultimate goal, even though we approach it from different vantage points. We are all looking for ways for vital organizations in our communities and in our society to have a broader impact. What that impact is will vary from organization to organization—from solving local social issues to addressing long-term environmental concerns to conducting medical research. The variety that makes the nonprofit sector such a vital element of our society is also what makes our work in improving effectiveness so complicated.

Since I joined GEO in 2001 I have met with many different players in pursuit of a strong, vibrant nonprofit sector. From my conversations with nonprofits, researchers, technical assistance providers, and funders, I have learned of various approaches to strengthening nonprofits. Combining these different experiences and vantage points makes GEO's work to clarify the language, expectations, and impact of improving organizations easier. While we may not have all the answers, we have learned that when it comes to improving nonprofit performance, one size truly does not fit all. Grantmakers are finding success in improving effectiveness through a variety of approaches that play to the strengths and needs of their own organizations and those of their nonprofit partners.

GEO's diverse membership represents a variety of approaches. These examples help highlight several ways funders can partner with nonprofits to strengthen organizations.

Multiple Approaches to Achieving Effectiveness

In *Strengthening Nonprofit Performance: A Funder's Guide to Capacity Building*, co-published by the Amherst H. Wilder Foundation and GEO, authors Paul Connolly and Carol Lukas outline specific approaches grantmakers can use to strengthen nonprofit organizations. These approaches fall into five broad categories:

- Direct support for organizational effectiveness
- General operating support grants
- Capital financing
- Support to infrastructure organizations and continual learning
- Technical assistance

Certainly some approaches can be equally effective without falling neatly into one of these categories, but this list provides a general framework that can guide grantmakers in their work with nonprofits. The following pages provide just a few of the hundreds of examples of funders who are achieving results through these approaches.

Direct Support for Organizational Effectiveness

One of the most common ways funders support nonprofits' effectiveness efforts is by providing grants specifically focused on strengthening organizations. Some funders make such support available exclusively to program area grantees. This can be done in a variety of ways. For example, the Mary Reynolds Babcock Foundation and the William Penn Foundation add a percentage to program grants for capacity building. Other grantmaking organizations have distinct organizational effectiveness programs. The Eugene and Agnes E. Meyer Foundation in Washington, D.C., created the Nonprofit Sector Advancement Fund in 1994 to strengthen the local nonprofit sector by improving organizational effectiveness through a variety of means including cash flow loans, management assistance, or general operating support.

"At the Meyer Foundation, we view capacity building as betting on the best nonprofit leaders in our region and finding ways to support sustainable work," said Julie L. Rogers, the foundation's president. "Building solid internal structures can make a significant difference in an organization's ability to sustain good programs."

Still other grantmakers, such as the Nonprofit Management Fund of Milwaukee, take a more specific approach. Started in 1994 as a demonstration project of three local foundations, the fund has since grown to include sixteen funding partners, including foundations, corporations, and the United Way. Collectively, the partners have made more than $3 million in grants to strengthen the management and governance of nonprofit organizations and increase the available resources for nonprofit management in the area.

"That these funders sit at the same table and make collective decisions about what to fund and how has had a tremendous impact on nonprofit organizations," said fund adviser Patricia Wyzbinski. "It has caused everyone to look at the nonprofit sector's needs in a new way, with an eye to how we, as funders, can help strengthen nonprofits together."

Grantmakers often can accomplish more through collaboration than by working alone. Working with other funders in a targeted, coordinated effort decreases duplication of efforts and helps minimize confusion on the part of nonprofits. From these sixteen funders, nonprofits receive one consistent description of effectiveness toward which to strive.

While technical assistance grants that build the capacity of individual nonprofit organizations represent the largest share of the fund's annual disbursements, the sponsoring organizations also are interested in making broader investments to improve the effectiveness of the local nonprofit sector as a whole. For example, the fund offers diagnostic clinics that provide a comprehensive analysis and recommendations on key performance issues, in lieu of a grant, for area nonprofits. The fund also has launched initiatives aimed at strengthening nonprofit boards, improving nonprofits' access to and understanding of technology, and promoting social entrepreneurship.

To the extent that a group of grantmakers shares a common goal of supporting performance improvement in a specific subset of nonprofit organizations—be it geographically bound, issue bound, or otherwise—this strategy leverages resources, provides a coordinated approach, and includes a variety of forms that could be replicated on as large or small a scale as necessary. Grantmakers do not need to establish stand-alone programs to support organizational effectiveness, and program staff do not need to be well versed in organizational theory, but staff should have at least some knowledge of organizational effectiveness. For example, program officers should build into their due diligence process a way to identify indicators of effective and less-than-effective organizations and work with these nonprofits accordingly.

When providing direct support for organizational effectiveness, funders do not need to work alone. As described later in this chapter and in the following chapters, they have a variety of opportunities for collaboration with other funders, consultants, or technical service providers.

Questions for Funders

- How do we integrate support for organizational effectiveness into our day-to-day grantmaking? What could we do differently?

- What assets do we have to successfully support organizational effectiveness? What areas could use further development?

- With whom could we partner to provide our nonprofit partners organizational effectiveness support?

General Operating Support

Another relatively easy strategy that funders large and small can adopt to support effectiveness is to provide general operating support. To ensure sustainability, nonprofits should have diversified funding and a healthy reserve fund—ideally enough to cover six months of operating expenses. The reality is that very few nonprofits are able to achieve this level of financial stability—in general, too much of their support comes with program restrictions. Funders can and should take some responsibility for helping nonprofits achieve this level of sustainability. Often, grantmakers prefer to provide program support rather than general operating support. If funders continue to place value on new or expanding programs without continuing to support those that are proven successful, nonprofits will need to add or expand programs in order to get grant dollars. At the very least, funders should be willing to provide *fully weighted program support*—meaning support that covers the administrative and operational costs of running the program. A preference for program grants, and more specifically for funding new programs, could encourage ill-conceived growth and a lack of focus in nonprofits. Chasing after program support may also provide nonprofits a disincentive to focus on core systems and infrastructure because they don't have enough money to pay for them.

Fortunately, many funders are seeing the problems providing only program support can cause, recognizing the need for general operating support, and giving it more frequently. They trust the nonprofits to set their own priorities and determine the best use of funds, and they work with grantees to determine appropriate ways to measure success for operating support. For example, the Edna McConnell Clark Foundation first provides support for comprehensive business planning before providing additional funding.

According to a report by The Foundation Center (2003), general support grants are on the rise—accounting for a record share in 2001. General support grant dollars increased by 27.1 percent between 2000 and 2001, while the number of general support grants grew by 5.5 percent. General support grants include funding for general operating support, as well as for management development, income development, and annual campaigns.

Although general operating support grants cover vital infrastructure expenses, they are often the most difficult dollars for nonprofits to raise, and program grants often do not adequately cover overhead expenses. Much of this responsibility lies with the grantees. Feeling pressure to run programs efficiently as they can, many nonprofits leave out overhead expenses in grant proposals. Nonprofits should fully weight grant applications to account for all overhead expenses so the program does not become a drain on their assets.

The California Wellness Foundation decided in 2000 to focus on giving core support to grantees. Guided by the premise that "individuals and organizations that work on the front line know best how resources need to be allocated to improve the health of the diverse populations in California," the new strategy has allowed the foundation to be more responsive to the needs of grantees. More than half the foundation's grant dollars cover general operating support.

During tough economic times, this strategy allowed TCWF to help organizations maintain their service levels and existing programs. While other funders were cutting back support due to diminishing endowments, the core support from TCWF allowed nonprofits to cover the costs of doing business, such as rent, fundraising expenses, and salaries.

Although providing core support gives nonprofits greater flexibility, many grantmakers can attest that the decision to give general operating support comes with a level of risk for both the funder and the grantee. Some nonprofits may not be at an appropriate stage to get a large general operating support grant because they may not have the management or practices in place to manage that grant effectively. To ensure the most effective use of grant dollars, TCWF staff members conduct a thorough due diligence process to ensure they pick the most appropriate partners.

"Sustainability is the goal of these grants from the outset," said president and CEO Gary Yates. "Our reviews of individual grants so far have indicated that core support dollars have been put to a variety of creative uses that have enhanced organizational effectiveness in ways we might not have originally anticipated. Rather than creating stress for organizations, our funding has served to strengthen their work."

Despite the benefits of providing general operating support, according to The Foundation Center (2003), the average general operating support grant amount—$108,636 in 2001—still lags behind the average program grant amount—$171,689 in 2001.

Some funders say general operating support grants make it somewhat harder to measure impact. When making general operating support grants, funders can't measure a direct effect on the organization's stakeholders, but they can look at business plans or organizational evaluations to ensure they are supporting strong programs that are in line with the funder's vision.

Questions for Funders

- How can we integrate general operating support into our regular grantmaking?

- Do our grantees account for an appropriate amount of overhead in their program proposals? How can we communicate differently with our grantees to help them understand our willingness to cover all expenses?

- What criteria are important as we consider providing general operating support? Some possibilities include length of relationship with the grantee, confidence in senior leadership, or the organization's performance track record.

Capital Financing

To run strong programs, nonprofits need adequate facilities and a strong, sustainable financial position. Providing capital financing can support the renovation, building, or acquisition of facilities for office space or program delivery or provide capital to help nonprofits cover expenses in the form of cash flow loans or program-related investments.

Capital financing often involves a higher level of engagement than other forms of effectiveness work. Through capital financing, funders are working to improve nonprofits' financial positions and institute sound financial management practices, so capital financing may be more time intensive and may require more financial resources.

Since 1983, National Arts Strategies (formerly National Arts Stabilization) has worked to reinvigorate local arts organizations through arts-capitalization strategies and capacity-building projects, executive education, community financial analyses, and research. The original model for community-based capitalization efforts was called "stabilization": a community-based collaborative effort of foundation, corporate, individual, and government donors, who invest in a multiyear program of grantmaking and technical assistance. The aim of the collaborative is to stabilize an organization with a strong financial profile consisting of an appropriate combination of three capitalization targets:

- *Working capital* (10 to 30 percent of annual operating expenses) to allow the organization to pay its bills on time.
- *Net assets invested in property and equipment* (dependent on the organization's investments) to meet the organization's need for buildings, equipment, and other fixed assets.
- *Assets invested as endowment* (200 to 500 percent of annual operating expenses to provide 10 to 25 percent of annual revenue) to help ensure long-term sustainability. This benchmark is tailored to the needs of each art form and to the cost of raising endowment funds.

In addition to providing grants for one or all of these capitalization areas, NAS also provides executive education and technical assistance to help staff and board members learn new management approaches and skills to help increase earned income, build endowments, and invest in infrastructure. NAS has found that once organizations have received this assistance, their managerial and fiscal fitness makes them more attractive to foundations and corporate donors who are committed to helping ensure long-term financial strength. Group learning opportunities for arts leaders in particular help to strengthen local communities.

"We have learned that knowledge capital and human capital can play as successful a part in the sustainability of an arts organization as working capital," said NAS president Russell Willis Taylor. "In other words, continued executive education and looking at how to retain the best people are key parts in reviewing the full resources of the organization. Money alone isn't enough."

Cash Flow Loans. Long-term sustainability is important, but sometimes organizations need emergency assistance to help them through cash flow challenges. To provide this sort of capital financing, the Meyer Foundation provides short-term, interest-free cash flow loans of up to $75,000. The loans are made on a first-come, first-served basis from a revolving fund of $1 million and are good for 30 to 180 days. These loans enable nonprofits to deliver programs and services to constituents and paychecks to employees without interruption during times when expected revenue is delayed.

Understanding that cash flow problems are emergencies that need to be addressed quickly, Meyer staff members strive to respond to every inquiry within one week. In addition to the loan, Meyer provides cash flow counseling to nonprofits to help prevent cash shortages from happening again.

Nonprofits say the cash flow loans can be lifesavers. One grantee nearly had to postpone the start of work on a new technology training center when a grant was delayed. A cash flow loan from

Meyer enabled the nonprofit to continue its work on a center that provides computer and telecommunications training. "Without support from the cash flow loan program, I would not have been able to keep my team intact," the executive director said.

"Our cash flow loan program is designed to help solid organizations that are caught in financial crises because of the funding environment," said Meyer Foundation president Julie L. Rogers. "We provide a loan when an organization's financial health is threatened by delays in expected revenue. What we have learned through our work with cash flow loans is that many nonprofits are not using all the tools available to them to ensure financial wellbeing. Through our cash flow loan program, Meyer has found an opportunity to educate organizations about important financial practices such as cash flow forecasting."

Program-Related Investments. Another way grantmakers can provide capital financing is through program-related investments. PRIs are loans to nonprofits that can come from the funder's investment corpus or from its grantmaking stream. The terms of the loan are up to the funder—PRIs are commonly repaid in three to five years, and interest rates are at the funder's discretion but are usually lower than market. PRIs can benefit both parties. Nonprofits receive access to capital at below-market rates, and funders get an opportunity to double their impact on nonprofits with the same amount of money. The PRI can count toward pay-out requirements only once. When the loan is repaid, the foundation must redistribute the money in excess of that year's 5 percent distribution, so the money invested in PRIs benefits nonprofits once in the initial loan and a second time after the loan is repaid and the money is paid out in the traditional grantmaking stream.

When considering making a PRI, funders should ask a few questions about the potential grantee:

- *Does the organization have good financial management and accounting in place?* Review financial statements closely to determine whether the organization has a stable financial history.

- *Will this loan help the nonprofit generate capital to repay the loan?* PRIs can best be used to help launch or expand business ventures or other revenue-earning programs. If the nonprofit wants to use the loan to finance day-to-day operations, a traditional grant may be more appropriate.
- *Does the nonprofit have sufficient assets in place to absorb any shocks?* Whether the organization is embarking on a capital project or developing a new program or business venture, financial challenges will probably arise along the way. Before making a PRI, make sure the nonprofit has lined up all the capital it requires to undertake the project.

Often grantmakers rely on intermediaries to administer PRIs, perform due diligence on candidates, and provide standard loan administration services. Some examples include the Calvert Foundation in Maryland and the Local Initiatives Support Corporation and Nonprofit Finance Fund, both in New York.

To evaluate the success of a PRI, funders should look at both the nonprofit's performance and financial stability. Success indicators include

- Ability to repay the loan
- Satisfactory levels of working capital reserves
- Current liquidity
- Increased earned income levels

Cash flow loans and program-related investments are among the riskier forms of support of nonprofits, because the recipients may not be able to repay the loan. To manage this risk, funders should conduct thorough due diligence of grantees to ensure they have sound finances and strong management.

Questions for Funders

- In what ways do we help our nonprofits improve sustainability and financial management?

- How can we be helpful to our nonprofit partners during financial emergencies?

- Are we prepared to take the risk of providing cash flow loans or program-related investments? Is this an option that should be made available to our grantees?

Supporting Infrastructure and Learning

When a company wants to rethink a process, engage in planning, launch a new IT system, or revamp its financial management practices, it often hires expert consultants from fairly high-cost firms—firms that are often out of reach for most nonprofits. Over the past two decades a parallel system of management support, education, and research has emerged and has become vital to the performance of the nonprofit sector. Today, some of the most important players in the organizational effectiveness field are the researchers, intermediaries, associations, and technical assistance providers dedicated to strengthening the sector. Often, these organizations are the ones looking out for the sector's best interests, highlighting its strengths, and striving for innovation and improvement. Without these intermediary organizations as a strong backbone for the sector, funders' work in improving effectiveness would be much more difficult.

Infrastructure and learning organizations come in a variety of forms:

- *Management support organizations* that work with nonprofits to provide technical assistance and support on a variety of issues. Examples include NPower, CompassPoint Nonprofit Services, or the Support Center of New York.

- *Nonprofit associations* that provide support, resources, and referrals for nonprofits based on region or type. Examples include the Council on Foundations, the American Society of Association Executives, the Museum Trustee Association, and the Ohio Association of Nonprofit Organizations.

- *Researchers and academic centers* that study the sector in search of promising practices. Examples include the Aspen Institute's Nonprofit Sector Research Fund, Harvard University's Hauser Center, the Brookings Institution, the Urban Institute, and Johns Hopkins University's Center for Civil Society Studies.

- *National infrastructure organizations* such as BoardSource, Independent Sector, and the Alliance for Nonprofit Management.

As part of its Strengthening U.S. Democracy program, Carnegie Corporation of New York invests in capacity building for groups of nonprofits at the state, regional, or national levels and focuses its support on intermediary organizations. Carnegie believes the nonprofit sector is essential to U.S. democracy and that it is critical to ensure it has the capacity to respond to new challenges while at the same time improving its effectiveness.

"Supporting the nonprofit sector's infrastructure is critical to its future health," said Cynthia Gibson, program officer of the Strengthening U.S. Democracy program. "If funders say they support effective organizations and capacity building, they should support the infrastructure behind it. Understandably, not all funders can—nor should they necessarily—support national intermediaries, but they can support the management support organizations, consultants, trainers, researchers, and others that are providing important capacity-building services to nonprofits in their cities, states, or regions."

The Meadows Foundation has a long history of providing capacity-building support to Texas nonprofits, perhaps most successfully by granting millions of dollars to create nonprofit service centers throughout the state. In the 1980s, the foundation's board found itself turning down proposals that had true potential because the organizations lacked the internal capacity to execute strong and sustainable programs.

"The foundation had limited resources," said Mike McCoy, senior program officer. "It pained the board to have to tell grantseekers they could not have funding because the organizations were lacking in governance, management, or financial oversight; yet there was nowhere to send these organizations to get the things they needed. The board thought, 'Wouldn't it be great if there was a place nonprofits could go to get high-caliber consulting services at an affordable price?' "

To address this need, the Meadows Foundation created the Center for Nonprofit Management in Dallas. The center was built on a model with three principles:

- Direct consultation to address individual organizational needs
- Workshops throughout the year that covered various topics from a broad-based perspective
- A telephone, online, or drop-in library resource so nonprofits could get information they needed quickly and inexpensively

After seeing the success of the Dallas center, the Meadows Foundation decided to establish a nonprofit center within a hundred-mile distance of every large city in Texas. Foundation staff convened nonprofit leaders, consultants, and funders in communities across the state to garner support for creating centers. Once the local nonprofit communities could create a plan for sustainability, the Meadows Foundation offered to help with start-up funds for the center. So far, the Meadows Foundation has established sixteen centers across Texas, all of which use the Meadows model.

In addition, the Meadows Foundation established The Texas Nonprofit Management Assistance Network, which provides technical assistance to the individual centers and networks the centers and other management support organizations. "This type of work should be at the core of every funder," McCoy said. "Our grants are only as good as the organizations that we support. Building the capacity of the nonprofit industry is at the core of what we do. Funders should always be thinking of ways to increase the capacity of recipients."

While many of the best-known infrastructure support organizations operate at the national level, many organizations and individuals are doing valuable work at the regional and local levels as well, so funders can find the appropriate level to support. Regardless of whether or how funders support these groups, any grantmakers that are truly committed to this work should be familiar with the resources available to their grantees—whether they be at the national or local level—and find ways to ensure they remain strong and valuable resources for nonprofits.

Questions for Funders

- How do we support the supporters of nonprofit infrastructure?
- How do we stay current with the forms of support available to our grantees?
- How do we ensure these resources remain valuable and helpful?

Technical Assistance

One of the most engaged forms of organizational effectiveness support funders can provide is technical assistance. This support can come in a variety of ways. Some funders provide the assistance themselves, others help nonprofits hire the right consultant, and yet others provide funding for technical assistance and let the nonprofits make the decisions on their own. Grantmakers can provide technical assistance independently or through a collaborative.

Robin Hood—a public charity created in 1988 by a group of Wall Street executives who wanted to adapt investment principles and business practices to charitable giving—fights poverty in New York by making grants and providing capacity-building services to local nonprofits. It selects programs that are most effective at helping the city's two million poor build better lives for themselves and their families. To date, Robin Hood has given more than $170 million in program grants and general operating support to its core portfolio organizations. Following the attacks on the World Trade Center in 2001, Robin Hood established a relief fund that has granted an additional $58.1 million to those affected by the attacks. Robin Hood's board of directors underwrites its administrative and fundraising expenses in full, so every penny contributed by the community goes directly to help those in poverty.

Robin Hood values long-term, engaged partnerships. It imposes no time limitations on funding, so annual turnover in the grant-making portfolio is low. Many grant recipients have been funded for more than ten years. In addition, Robin Hood provides capacity-building services tailored to meet the needs of individual grantees and secures in-kind donations of goods and services. In-house general management consultants and experts from some of New York's top professional services firms provide management assistance in a variety of areas including strategic planning, board development, fiscal management, and technology. In 2002, capacity building provided to grant recipients by staff and donated by professional service firms was valued at more than $2.7 million.

"Leaders of social service nonprofits have to manage complex organizations, usually without the resources of their peers in business," said Michael Park, Robin Hood's director of management assistance. "We help them access the highest-quality intensive consulting services available in the market, remove the barriers of cost, and thus help them do better what they already do well—save lives. It's wonderful to see the impact of this work several years out—an agency we helped with strategic planning, which grew as a result of their plan and now needs a more sophisticated level of accounting administration to manage the growth they have achieved."

In a survey conducted in 2001 by McKinsey & Company, 85 percent of Robin Hood grant recipients said the assistance they received helped build long-term capacity within their organizations. Grantees ranked management assistance as the second most valuable service the foundation offered—funding was ranked first.

Another collaborative, Nonprofit Support Center, was created to provide technical assistance to nonprofits. In 1991, three nonprofit organizations in Worcester, Massachusetts, saw a need to help county nonprofit leaders manage their limited resources more effectively and creatively. The result was the Coalition for Not-for-Profit Management Assistance, a collaboration of the Greater Worcester Community Foundation, the United Way of Central Massachusetts, and the Colleges of Worcester Consortium. In its early years, the organization offered occasional seminars and community volunteers provided management support to individual organizations.

In 1998, reflecting the increasing number and expanding scope of its services, the organization changed its name to the Nonprofit Support Center. It is now a project of the Greater Worcester Community Foundation and is guided by an advisory committee of nonprofit executive directors, funders, and consultants. One of the signature goals of the Center, according to Gail Randall, the special projects officer in charge, is to advance peer learning among area nonprofits.

"The Nonprofit Support Center exists to build a collaborative nonprofit sector in Central Massachusetts," Randall said. "We see that as a key to our mission: To help people get to know each other, learn together, and develop the relationships that create a tightly knit and cooperative sector."

The Center provides executive directors and organizational teams with opportunities for in-depth course work and the chance to investigate important issues both with high-caliber presenters and with peers. "We're finding more and more that we want to focus on peer learning because that's where substantive change takes place," Randall said. "We think learning becomes institutionalized when you have opportunities to continue the conversation with people nearby." Courses offered have focused on strategic technology use, fund development, board recruitment, and how to be successful in today's uncertain environment. A management institute for executive directors and a workshop exclusively for board chairs are provided on a regular basis.

In other activities, the Nonprofit Support Center has a small pool of money to help nonprofit organizations manage change and growth. Funds are used to support consultant fees. The center also provides organizational assessment services and resource and referral assistance, in part because Massachusetts does not have a state association of nonprofits.

Although providing technical assistance can be one of the most difficult capacity-building strategies to adopt, funders opting not to offer technical assistance should ensure grantees have another resource to go to for help. Funders that directly provide technical assistance should have staff with expertise in organizational development or a strong relationship with a consultant or other technical service provider.

Questions for Funders

- How can we most effectively facilitate nonprofits' receiving technical assistance?
- In our community, what areas are lacking in technical expertise?

Grantmakers Can't Be Everything to Everyone

With a wide variety of possible approaches to improving effectiveness and many different needs from grantees, strengthening nonprofits can be a daunting task indeed. To improve chances of success, funders should not try to be everything to everyone. Instead, grantmakers can work most effectively by finding a niche they can serve well and seeking nonprofit partners with needs inside that niche. Funders can find this niche in two ways:

- Focusing internally on the funder's strengths and finding grantees with needs in that niche
- Listening to the needs of nonprofits in the community and developing skills to serve those needs

Focusing on Strengths

Although a few of the largest foundations may have the experience and resources necessary to provide a variety of capacity-building approaches to grantees, most grantmaking organizations have limited budgets and staff. Thus the majority can work most effectively by focusing on a few core programs and doing them well or by collaborating with other funders to provide a comprehensive set of services.

The possible danger in this approach is that funders can become too internally focused and try to shoehorn grantees into existing programs without carefully considering whether the funder's strengths and the grantee's needs are an appropriate match. Nonetheless, funders who focus on one or a few specific programs have as much chance to succeed in their chosen realm as a large foundation with national programs in a variety of areas would have with any given program. The smaller funders might just need to spend more time searching for the appropriate grantees.

The Taproot Foundation was established in 2001. Unlike other foundations, which start out with a financial endowment, Taproot has an endowment that consists of a network of business professionals with skills in demand from local nonprofit organizations. The Taproot Foundation acts as a contractor—creating and managing teams of volunteers on multi-month projects helping to build the infrastructure of an organization. The Taproot Foundation coined the term *service grants* to describe these projects, which are competitively awarded to organizations through a standard grantmaking process. The Taproot Foundation started in San Francisco; it began a pilot program in New York in 2003 and intends to roll out its service grant program nationally.

"With the downturn in the economy, nonprofits are facing increased demand for their services and at the same time are seeing public and private funding for their services greatly reduced," said Aaron Hurst, president of the Taproot Foundation. "To survive, nonprofits must reduce their costs by increasing their efficiency and are forced to rely more heavily on donations from individuals rather than institutions. Our service grant program is designed to help them weather the storm and achieve their goals."

Responding to Nonprofits' Needs

Other grantmakers, particularly those serving local nonprofits, may find it more effective to determine nonprofits' needs in improving effectiveness and develop programs or skills to help meet those needs.

The Nokomis Foundation provides funding, resources, and expertise for organizations to make a difference in the lives of women and girls. The foundation focuses on organizations primarily working in Kent, Ottawa, and Allegan counties in West Michigan.

In 2000, when foundation staff determined that a majority of grantees could use help improving their use of technology, the foundation established a technology consortium to build staff and organizational capacity and increase nonprofits' access to and use of technology. The foundation selected twelve partner organizations, all women-run and serving women or girls, with budgets ranging from $105,000 to $3.8 million. The intent of the consortium was to build a stronger network among partner organizations and share resources. The Nokomis Foundation is now in year four of a projected five-year commitment to providing staff assistance and funding, technical assistance sessions, and training and networking opportunities. Originally Nokomis envisioned a two-year project but extended it based on feedback from grantees.

As a result of the consortium, participating nonprofits were able to save on hardware and software expenses through collective purchasing. In addition, individuals reported improved technology skills and more networking with colleagues, while organizations reported a firmer conviction to investing in technology and more creative approaches to finding technology solutions.

"The Technology Consortium has been more effective than we ever imagined," said Kym Mulhern, Nokomis Foundation president and CEO. "Initially we were hoping to build the technological capacity of individual organizations. Now we can see the consortium has also built the capacity of participants to collaborate, network, communicate, and advocate."

The consortium was a learning opportunity for Nokomis Foundation staff as well. With a staff of two full-time employees and one part-time, the foundation often found it difficult to make use of technology a priority over programmatic issues. From the consortium, Nokomis Foundation staff realized the importance of devoting money and time to learning ways to use technology better—not only to help them do their work more efficiently, but so they could set an example for their nonprofit partners.

An Exception to the Rule

Although many grantmaking organizations work most effectively by focusing on a few specific programs or approaches, some funders do provide various forms of support to help improve nonprofits' effectiveness based on their individual needs. One example is the Local Initiatives Support Corporation, based in New York, with thirty-eight local offices across the country.

LISC provides broad-based support to a select audience—more than eighteen hundred community development corporations (CDCs). In partnership with their Organizational Development Initiative, LISC program staff created *Cap*Map™, a developmental growth model and diagnostic tool designed to assist them in mapping the current capacity of an organization, working in partnership with a CDC to determine a path for growth, and measuring achievement along the way.

Based on the guiding principle that organizations are dynamic entities that can be masterful in one area yet weak in another, despite organizational longevity, *Cap*Map distinguishes progressive stages of competency in nine key areas of organizational activity LISC considers crucial for success:

- Board governance
- Community connections
- Executive director
- Financial management
- Fund development
- Human resources and staff development
- Management information systems
- Real estate asset management
- Real estate development

Focusing on what is present and possible rather than missing or deficient in an organization, the capacity mapping approach is a collaborative five-step process:

1. Identify the key areas and stages of competency needed for an organization to achieve its unique vision.
2. Use *Cap*Map to establish a baseline measurement of the organization's current level of capacity in each key area.

3. Compare the ideal (as identified in step 1) with the real (identified in step 2) and establish a comprehensive growth plan to move the organization progressively through increasing stages of capacity in each key area.

4. Assist the organization in accessing the capacity-building resources needed to implement the plan.

5. Use CapMap again after a predetermined period of time to measure actual capacity growth and verify impact.

By using CapMap to help target and refine strategies for organizational growth, and—most important—to consistently measure progress with a common yardstick, LISC strives to work more effectively with its CDC partners. "Our hope is that CapMap will assist in identifying specific areas of organizational growth to invest in, planning the use of resources more effectively, and evaluating the impact of our capacity building efforts," said Maria Gutierrez, vice president of LISC. So far the results have been positive. "We are excited about the statistically significant data that is coming out of this effort. In the near future, we hope to share important and, for the first time, empirical information with the rest of the nonprofit sector about how organizations grow, and what capacity-building investments are most effective in helping them achieve powerful results."

"The capacity-mapping process was an eye opener that has led to additional analysis of our financial management systems, the purchase and implementation of more relevant software, and the ability to access better information," said Willie Logan, president of Opa-Locka Community Development Corporation in Miami.

Conclusion

The organizational effectiveness field is broad and complex. Every nonprofit facing an effectiveness challenge needs its own unique solution. Grantmakers with limited resources and focused visions cannot solve every effectiveness challenge. However, this should not discourage funders from trying to strengthen the nonprofit sector. Key to being a good partner is knowing where your organization is best positioned to help and partnering with fellow grantmakers to meet the multitude of needs nonprofits face.

By sharing knowledge and experience with one another, grantmakers can learn promising practices and new approaches, thereby building upon the knowledge of others in the field to determine appropriate methods and strategies in their own work. Granted, there will still be some unsuccessful grants or some capacity-building projects that flounder, but by focusing on their strengths and creating a niche for successful capacity-building work, grantmakers can have real and lasting impact that will ripple throughout the sector.

Chapter Three

Setting Clear Goals with High Expectations

Janine E. Lee, Vice President, Youth Development Division, Ewing Marion Kauffman Foundation

It has been said that the first law of philanthropy, like the first law of medicine, is "Do No Harm." According to Payton (1988), "The best philanthropy, the help that does the most good and the least harm, the help that nourishes civilization at its very root . . . is not what is usually called charity. . . . [It is] the investment of effort or time or money . . . to expand and develop resources at hand and to give opportunity for progress and helpful labor where it did not exist before. No mere money-giving is comparable to this in its lasting and beneficial results."

The philanthropic sector is traditionally known for providing resources in specific, designated nonprofit programs, not in general operations. However, providing all program support and no infrastructure support could end up being more harmful than helpful. According to one group of researchers, "the day-to-day grantmaking practices of many foundations actually undermine the ability of nonprofits to develop the capacity for sustained high performance" (Letts, Ryan, and Grossman, 1999). The group noted several concerns:

- Funders are making mostly targeted grants that support specific programs and not investing in the infrastructure that ensures these programs can be delivered.
- Funders will have to conquer the traditional nonprofit overhead phobia and consider how they might expand their own organizational capacity or restructure their grantmaking operations.

- Sweeping social change goals will need to be converted into a series of clear interim results that the grantee and funder can work toward together.

For years the leaders of nonprofit organizations labored every day just to keep from stalling, struggling to accomplish worthy tasks with inadequate resources to get the job done. Today those nonprofit leaders use new engines to drive programs that fulfill their missions. They manage ongoing professional concerns, balancing sophisticated bottom-line business discipline with unrelenting societal needs. They defy business logic by embracing endeavors that are the least likely to provide a lucrative return.

"The organizational effectiveness initiative really does away with the old-school thinking around how nonprofits ought to operate and be administered," says David Smith, president of the Boys and Girls Clubs of Greater Kansas City.

"The old thinking was that nonprofits weren't supposed to make money or carry over a portion of their budget. They were supposed to spend everything they brought in and go to a zero balance at the end of the year," says Richard Ruiz, executive director of El Centro in Kansas City, Kansas. "Nonprofits were supposed to rely on the generosity of others in order to deal with community issues. Some of that behavior and attitude still exist, but the more we talk about social entrepreneurship, those attitudes are changing, making our industry more responsible, accountable, and exciting."

Left to decipher ways to apply business lessons to their life's work, nonprofit leaders are expected to be better managers, have a clear sense of their goals, understand competition, measure results, and be accountable for the successes and shortfalls of their product. This may mean breaking with custom or comfort to accept risk, welcome new collaborative partners, or consider innovative exercises that will build the entrepreneurial muscle and create vibrant social enterprises with staying power.

Grantmakers—also working to realize a mission and vision—can achieve their philanthropic purposes only through the work of their service delivery system, the nonprofit sector. This interdependent relationship calls for both parties to have a deep understanding of each other's needs and expectations, and to agree upon mutually shared goals.

On the surface, identifying these goals may seem simple. In most cases the goal of a grantmaker is to achieve social change by improving the ability of a nonprofit to fulfill a mission that is aligned with the vision of the grantmaker. But how does a grantmaker best improve a nonprofit's ability to improve its mission? By supporting new programs? Building infrastructure? Creating an endowment? As the examples in Chapter Two illustrate, grantmakers face choices among numerous ways to achieve desired impact. After selecting a specific strategy, a grantmaker still must choose how to implement that strategy to achieve the desired goal.

In their day-to-day work, funders should work in collaboration with grantees to determine what type of support would be most beneficial. In their long-term vision and planning, grantmakers should look critically at the impact of changes on the nonprofit sector as a whole as well as on individual grantees and should determine how to stay adaptable to meet these changing needs.

The Ewing Marion Kauffman Foundation is a firm believer in the principle that a funder can expand its impact by working with nonprofit partners to strengthen organizations' internal capacities. However, as earlier chapters in this book have suggested, *building capacity* means different things to different organizations and can be a complicated process.

In the for-profit sector, the bottom line is clearly described as profit and increasing shareholder value. In the nonprofit sector, the bottom line is not so easily defined. Sullivan (1995) emphasizes the implications of this lack of a clear criterion, noting that nonprofits "must develop other measures by which to assess their performance." But, as Sullivan notes, this task is challenging for nonprofit managers. Their organizations have multiple goals and stakeholders with sometimes conflicting objectives, and their focus on service delivery makes it difficult to assess the overall performance of their activities.

The nonprofit sector literature includes significant debate regarding the following issues:

- Competing models that attempt to define effectiveness
- Confusion about who the customer is (whether the client, the funder, or the broader community)
- Differing goals of various stakeholders

Determining what makes organizations effective is often referred to as an elusive task. Daniel Forbes (1997) describes organizational effectiveness as a powerful and problematic concept. *Powerful* in the sense that it represents a tool for evaluating and enhancing the work, and *problematic* in the sense that it means different things to different people. In a recent study completed to investigate stakeholder judgment of nonprofit charitable organization effectiveness, Herman and Renz (1999) note that the tendency of nonprofit managers to cite "doing things right" as an indicator of effectiveness "reinforces the view that nonprofit charities are not (and perhaps cannot be) comparatively assessed on bottom-line measures."

In the course of developing a framework for the Kauffman Foundation's organizational effectiveness grantmaking, I had the privilege of interviewing Dr. John Gardner to learn his thoughts on what makes nonprofits effective. Here is part of what he had to say on the subject:

> Generally, the experts go straight to matters of mission, structure, et cetera, and I'm going to say that the number one point is *good people*. And I mean good at the trustee level, at the executive level, the staff, generally. I don't mean high IQ or SAT scores or grade point average or graduate degrees from elite universities. I'm talking about to the extent that people are well equipped to do their jobs. I remember a situation in which a division of an organization I was running was in trouble. I really thought of abolishing the division. I thought, "Well, maybe it isn't well conceived. It just seems to get

us into trouble all the time." I got a new person to head it. The problems disappeared. I've seen that over and over again when you get the right person in the right job. And the wrong person in the job may be very able; great for some other job, but not necessarily for this one.

The second thing that strikes me is that the effective organization must *have the philosophy of renewal* and *practice renewal*. The challenges of tomorrow are not the same as the challenges of yesterday. And the world changes. It's changing all the time. If the organization doesn't change with it, it's headed for the dust pan of history. That means, by the way, having within it individuals who are renewing themselves. It's been my experience that individuals who have not renewed themselves or aren't in the habit of renewing themselves develop protections against that tumultuous world out there, and the protections are bureaucratic rules and rigidities and walls to protect their turf and all the things you associate with bureaucracy built by people who are afraid. They're afraid they are not equal to the challenges. And people who are renewing themselves just don't feel that way. They're not building walls. They are reaching out for the future.

The third one that is immensely important today is *skill and collaboration*. No nonprofit can work alone anymore. It used to be that you'd have these great old traditional nonprofits that saw their turf as sacred, and they operated more or less alone. It doesn't work that way anymore. The nonprofits have to know how to work with the local government, all levels of government, really. They have to know how to work with the corporations, the faith community, with other nonprofits in partnerships that meet the needs of the particular problem they are trying to solve.

Fourth, I would say, and most people would put this first, is it's got to be *well managed*. It's heartbreaking to see a well-meaning nonprofit fighting to accomplish a task with inadequate money to do it, and yet wasting the money it has because it isn't effectively managed. It's crucial that they learn how to manage their resources and do their job in an effective way.

The next point, I think an effective nonprofit has to *know how to serve its constituents*. We tend to think about our methods of doing things as an organization, meeting the next appointment and all that, and we forget that the main thing is that this organization is designed to serve somebody. Sometimes this gets oversimplified, because you know the customer isn't always right. Your constituents are apt to focus on short-term goals. Effective leaders want to serve the short-term goals, but they also realize there are long-term goals they'd better be paying attention to. If organizations run it all by public opinion polls, they may miss some of those long-term goals.

The last one is *outcome oriented*, and here again we have a wonderfully healthy idea that can be oversimplified. It really developed as a contrast to input oriented. Thirty years ago, organizations generally described their achievements by what they put into an effort. "How much money did we spend on it?" "How many people did we put on it?" "How many hours, man hours, did we devote to it?" And we finally woke up, certainly in the last fifteen to twenty years, to the fact that we'd better ask ourselves what that money was buying, and what those people were accomplishing, et cetera. So now we set out to measure outcomes. But again, in all this capacity to oversimplify things, we begin to say well you've got to measure the outcome, and if it isn't quantifiable and doesn't show up, you haven't done a good job. And this just flies in the face of the fact that some outcomes are not measurable.

An Alternative to the Bottom Line

In our work to strengthen the effectiveness of our nonprofit partners, we at the Kauffman Foundation have learned one central principle: *Success in this field relies on clear goals and expectations between funders and nonprofits*.

To ensure clear communications with our nonprofit partners, we conducted extensive research and interviews with grantees to create a framework to shape our grantmaking for organizational effectiveness. The resulting framework is a list of common attributes we have seen in our most effective nonprofit partners. Other funders may describe effective organizations in their own terms, but we look for organizations that are mission directed and vision driven, outcomes oriented, sustainable, entrepreneurial, adaptable, and customer focused.

Our work to create clear goals and expectations was guided by three core lessons:

- Clearly articulate your values, beliefs, and core purpose and develop relationships with nonprofits that are aligned with those beliefs.

- Communicate with nonprofits what you are hoping to accomplish through your grantmaking strategies in capacity building.

- When working to improve effectiveness, create clear criteria to which nonprofits can aspire.

Clear Statement of Beliefs

Clearly articulate your values, beliefs, and core purpose and develop relationships with nonprofits that are aligned with those beliefs.

For example, the mission of the Kauffman Foundation is to research and identify the unfulfilled needs of society and to develop, implement, and fund breakthrough solutions that have a lasting impact and offer a choice and hope for the future. The vision is "self-sufficient people in healthy communities."

These statements of philosophy are key to gaining an understanding of the foundation's commitment to organizational effectiveness today.

Our shared values are built around having genuine humility, being conscious of one's own limitations, being aware that money does not confer wisdom, and appreciating the importance of ongoing learning. Mr. Kauffman attributed his success to three key principles that guided his efforts, and foundation board and staff members strive to uphold these values and beliefs:

- It is best to treat others as we want to be treated, with humility, dignity, respect, and honesty.
- Effectiveness is based on relationships characterized by mutual trust and integrity.
- Responsible risk taking and lifelong learning are essential for personal and organizational learning, as is the importance of giving back to the community.

The Kauffman Foundation, like many foundations and other nonprofit organizations, is concerned about demonstrating that our work benefits the community through strategic outcomes. We realize we cannot achieve these outcomes without a delivery system, therefore we rely heavily on the ability of nonprofits to perform at high levels of effectiveness to achieve mutually beneficial goals. To continue this grantmaking approach, it is important that we work closely with our nonprofit partners to identify and support qualitative and, when possible, quantitative evaluation processes to monitor progress.

Questions for Funders

- Are our mission, vision, and goals clearly communicated to our grantees?
- Do we partner with organizations whose missions are aligned with our beliefs?

Clear Communications

Communicate to nonprofits what you are hoping to accomplish through your grantmaking strategies in capacity building.

The Kauffman Foundation applied this principle by identifying a list of key attributes of effective nonprofit organizations, based on input from nonprofit leaders locally and across the country. This list provided some context to our understanding of organizational effectiveness and strengthened communications with our grantees. It was critical to providing a framework for communicating how our grants are adding value to the improvement of outcomes for children, youth, and families.

Having this framework allowed us to make better investment decisions regarding our organizational effectiveness strategy, to recognize and share the lessons learned from the nonprofits that demonstrate effectiveness in one or more of the attributes identified, and to track our own progress. We were particularly interested in finding out if the attributes identified, and the supporting indicators of each, could assist us in evaluating whether we contributed to any increase in organizational capacity, strength, and performance. In the last analysis, the final measure of success would be to determine whether the increased capacity could be linked to improved outcomes for children, youth, and families in Kansas City.

The goals of refining our investment strategy and sharing lessons learned turned out to be much easier to achieve than the goal of assessing our success on the ground. The Kauffman Foundation has used the framework to develop grant guidelines and a request for proposals and to award grants that provide general operating funds and capacity-building support to nonprofit partners as investments toward the sustainability and growth of the organization. In addition, we established the REACH Award (Reaching for

Excellence Achieving Community Health) to recognize excellence in nonprofit organizational effectiveness. The REACH Award acknowledges organizations that have attained a level of excellence in one or more attributes, while they continue to strive to achieve a level of excellence in other attributes. In terms of evaluation, we are developing an organizational assessment using the attributes that we hope can serve as a learning tool for nonprofits.

Some would argue that such frameworks are counterproductive, given the heterogeneity of the nonprofit sector. Others argue that true effectiveness is best understood in a more contingent manner, based possibly upon stakeholder expectations or a given stage in the organization's life. Herman and Renz (1999) contend that one of the challenges of developing a framework of anything is that the more effectively it represents reality, the more complicated the framework becomes.

How can we develop a framework that captures the essence of effectiveness in nonprofits in a way that still keeps it simple enough to understand and analyze? Herman and Renz provided a set of critical questions that we considered when developing our own framework:

- Is it intended to be all-inclusive or illustrative?
- How should the categories identified in the framework relate to each other?
- Are they intended to be equally important? Interdependent or independent?
- Are some more important than others? Is there interaction among the categories?
- If an organization were judged to be high on only a few indicators, would it be considered less effective?

These questions highlight both the opportunities and the limitations of developing such frameworks. In answer to the questions, the Kauffman Foundation's framework is intended to be illustrative, with all the attributes being interdependent and equally important. While some attributes may stay the same, we recognize that they may change over time given the exponential environmental changes affecting the nonprofit sector, as well as the changing needs of the client or customer.

Regarding the effectiveness of nonprofits, our assumptions are the following:

- Behind every successful program is an organization that performs well.
- Programs alone are not key determinants of outcomes.
- The organization is more than a place where programs get delivered.
- Building strong organizations and programs that are aligned with the mission are the key to delivery on the organization's outcomes.
- "Value" is defined by the stakeholders (clients, funders, and the community).
- Effective financial management alone, while necessary, is not sufficient as an indicator of organizational effectiveness.

Questions for Funders

- Is our capacity-building approach informed by research?
- Have we gathered input from nonprofit leaders?
- How do we define capacity building?

Clear Criteria

When working to improve effectiveness, create clear criteria to which nonprofits can aspire.

Language makes a difference in this field: people talk constantly about *effectiveness* and *capacity* and the like, but their perceptions of what these terms mean vary a great deal. As noted earlier, the Kauffman Foundation defines effective nonprofits as those that blend a set of attributes throughout their operations. For each attribute we have created a set of supporting indicators to ensure that we and our grantees are using a shared language:

Attribute	*Sample Indicators*
Mission directed and vision driven	Mission and vision statements are clearly written and widely distributed.
Outcomes oriented	Desired outcomes are stated specifically and when possible in measurable terms.
	Outcome achievement is tracked over time, and assessed for corresponding improvements in the situation of the organization's stakeholders.
Sustainable	An effective long-term strategy has developed (or is in the process of developing) a diverse and stable funding base.
	The organization has six months' operating funds in reserve.
Entrepreneurial	The leadership exemplifies the values of the organization and the community.
	The organization pursues new opportunities and resources.

Attribute	Sample Indicators
Adaptable	The organization monitors changes in staff, clients, funding sources, legal requirements, and community needs.
	Response is smooth and appropriate whether changes are gradual or abrupt.
Customer focused	The organization knows its clientele and provides services they really want.
	The premises reflect respect for the clientele.

The following sections discuss the attributes and supporting indicators in detail, along with questions grantmakers can ask as they develop a shared language in their own work with nonprofits. In addition, vignettes profile the stories of a variety of Kansas City area nonprofit organizations, their experiences moving toward the performance indicators for each attribute of organizational effectiveness, and the lessons that developed along the way.

The Criteria in Action

Nonprofit leaders in Kansas City have used the six attributes of organizational effectiveness to structure board meeting agendas, set performance criteria and accountability measures, and create employee training and recognition programs based on the concepts. With the indicators before them, they have charted their own creative course to strengthen their organizations and ultimately improve the lives of children, youth, and families in Kansas City.

Effective Nonprofits Are Mission-Driven

Mission matters. The organization's mission and vision statements should be clearly written and known by staff and customers. These statements should be prominently displayed wherever the organization does business and should be printed on the organization's letterhead. The mission and vision statement should be broad enough to provide inspiration and specific enough to offer guidance to the organization in setting broad policy and making day-to-day decisions. Mechanisms should be in place to ensure that decisions are made in alignment with the mission.

A good mission statement should be succinct and strategic. The resulting outline of the nonprofit's purpose and philosophy should identify the uniqueness of the organization. And it should provide the overall direction guiding the development of the organization's principles, its goals, and its strategic objectives—the targets for the organization's primary activities.

Kansas City nonprofit leaders were clearly aware of the need for the mission to be tied to a market. They discussed the need to be flexible and market-driven to be effective. Stevens (1999) asserts that while the mission is important, every mission needs a market to provide its reason for being: "Mission can't exist without market."

Profile of a Mission-Driven Organization— Boys and Girls Clubs of Greater Kansas City

The mission statement of the Boys and Girls Clubs of Greater Kansas City is everywhere throughout the clubs and extended-day school sites. It appears along with the eighty-nine-year-old organization's familiar interlocking-hands logo in publications, bookmarks, and wallet cards. However, the place where Boys and Girls Clubs president David Smith most wants to see the organization's mission is in the actions of his associates.

A strategic planning process at the Boys and Girls Clubs has honed the organization's mission and vision into a set of core values and a comprehensive work plan. A three-inch-thick binder bulges with the complete plan, including specific goals, priorities, and dates, and the action sheets for the work of the organization. The staff participates in role-playing exercises to apply the mission and act out the organization's core values. The organization is even set up so that one associate can present a certificate to another to acknowledge someone who demonstrates the organization's values.

The system that seems so tidy today did not fall neatly into place. It took some messy sessions over seven years to drill to the core of the organization's values. "I'm not ashamed to admit that it took a long time for the organization to develop a clear set of core values," Smith said. "I don't know if we could have fully embraced a set of values any earlier."

Questions for Funders

- Does the organization use its mission statement as a criterion for determining success?

- Are mission and vision statements communicated throughout the organization and prominently displayed?

- Do actions and programs of the organization reflect the mission and vision statements?

- Are procedures in place for the review of the mission statements at appropriate intervals? Can the organization demonstrate that it reviews its mission and vision statements at regular intervals and makes necessary adaptations that support its strategic plan?

- Can the organization document how its strategic and business plans are aligned with its mission?

Effective Nonprofits Are Outcomes Oriented

An outcomes-oriented organization can describe the expected outcomes of its services in concrete, realistic terms. It recognizes that while measurement is important when possible, not all outcomes are measurable, particularly in complex human service delivery areas. Documentation of stories, lessons learned, and legends become an important part of the learning experience.

An outcomes-oriented organization focuses on outcomes that are operationally defined and where possible are measurable. The outcomes measured are logically related to the mission and the services provided. The organization makes a clear distinction between the process of service delivery, the outcomes, and the observable results of those services. Organizations in the human service discipline are now expected to show how their programs make a positive difference in the lives of their clients.

The organization should have a process in place to assess whether the outcomes are achieved. The leadership of the organization should use the resulting information to improve the services delivered and plan for the future. The organization should have a history of its own performance and comparable data (benchmarking) in its decision-making process.

Profile of an Outcomes-Oriented Organization: YMCA of Greater Kansas City

"The outcomes issue came at a time when we were being pressured to prove ourselves. In grant-funded programs we always had to prove the value of our work. In our fee-for-service programs we didn't have that. We didn't look intentional," said Gene Dooley, president of the YMCA of Greater Kansas City.

The outcomes-oriented approach worked itself into the YMCA's organizational culture over several years. The organization had been part of an outcomes-based pilot program for the national YMCAs and was selected to be an early Kansas City model for outcomes-based evaluation initiated by the Heart of America United Way. "It was a new way of thinking," Dooley said. "We had to get our egos out of the way and embrace it, understand it, and apply it to our work."

The outcomes planning concept was introduced at staff assemblies throughout the organization. Budgets and goals for the year 2000 were based on these outcomes, and each individual's performance review and job description included outcomes language.

"Outcomes-oriented evaluation has become the basis for the way we operate," Dooley said. "It's how we evaluate staff and make expenditure decisions. We know we're making headway when a youth sports director talks more about the developmental process than the results of a game."

Questions for Funders

- Are procedures in place to measure program and organizational outcomes?

- Does a strategic plan guide the organization?

- Does the organization evaluate outcomes in ways that are innovative and useful for guiding decision making by program leadership and funders?

- Does the organization document the connections between the mission and outcomes?

Effective Nonprofits Are Sustainable

If the changes in the economy in recent years have taught us any-thing, it is the importance of a diverse funding base and adequate reserves. In addition to developing earned-income strategies to decrease dependence on outside funding, nonprofits should strive to have six months of operating expenses in reserve funds to help them weather hard times in the future. However, creating a diverse and stable financial base is often one of the most challenging tasks nonprofits face. To become sustainable, long-term strategy is key.

The definition of sustainability for nonprofits draws challenge and debate. The most common definition or description typically focuses on financial or fund development capability. As one exec-utive stated, "Money is the coin upon which we are allowed to do our work." While executives were clear about the need for increased financial support from a variety of sources, many wanted to see an expanded definition to include the importance of the organization being market-driven, customer-driven, and focused on improving outcomes for the end user, which was described as the social return on investment, or SROI.

According to Stevens (1999), smart nonprofits know the value of carryover surpluses (excess revenue) to their ongoing fiscal sta-bility. Anticipating unstable conditions and inevitable changing circumstances is a sign of smart money management. As philan-thropic dollars get tighter, contributors will invest in organizations that have a chance of being around for a while, rather than those that consistently have a deficit.

Profile of a Sustainable Organization: DeLaSalle Education Center

Like many nonprofits, DeLaSalle Education Center found its finan-cial burden a daily struggle for many years. The real squeeze came when government funding streams, which had been providing nearly 80 percent of the organization's budget, were reduced to a trickle. "We went through a crisis in the mid-1980s. We really weren't managing. We were running around raising money for the next day's bills and the next week's payroll. We were fairly good at operating in a crisis, but it was deeply troubling. We really had to get our act together," said Executive Director Jim Dougherty.

DeLaSalle's board finance committee set a new standard for operating the nonprofit, working with the staff to develop the center's first long-term strategic plan designed to generate operating reserves. A computer replaced the agency's handwritten ledger book. The school purchased its building, developed a capital campaign for renovations, and kept the organization afloat by funding depreciation. "We were coming out of the woods. The long-range planning changed our scope dramatically," Dougherty said.

DeLaSalle's road to sustainability has allowed the nonprofit to consider new enterprises that were always out of reach before. The school's leadership decided against a charter school option but has opened its first middle school.

"I think this is the ultimate payoff for being a sustainable organization," Dougherty said. "We could take our time to work through the pros and cons of decisions. We went through a lot of soul-searching, and we will continue to review our options. Sustainability has given us the opportunity to stay focused on the attributes of our education process and take our mission a step further. We've been able to go way beyond ourselves."

Questions for Funders

- Does the organization have diverse funding sources so it is not overly dependent on a single funding source?

- Are appropriate financial controls established and followed within the organization?

- Are financial crises—unpredictable events that are beyond the control of the organization—managed?

- Has the organization's leadership, as a matter of written policy, established a reserve fund sufficient to cover the organization's operating expenses for a planned period of time?

Effective Nonprofits Are Entrepreneurial

The leaders of entrepreneurial organizations, at the board and staff levels, are dynamic and innovative. Their pursuit of mission-directed innovation is continuous. The leadership has a strong history of seeking new opportunities for the organization and new resources to address the challenges faced by the organization. They motivate and inspire others to high levels of performance. The executive leaders, board members, staff, and volunteers demonstrate high levels of integrity and ethics and are held in high esteem by everyone associated with the organization.

The leadership of an entrepreneurial organization exemplifies the values of the organization and the community. They inspire, motivate, and instruct the staff to high levels of performance. They are effective and persuasive communicators. They are committed to the public good and are wise stewards of the resources entrusted to the organization. These leaders have a clear vision for the future of the organization and effectively communicate their vision to others. They are innovative and able to manage the risks associated with the organization. They find and make wise use of resources from a variety of sources to expand and improve the services provided by the organization.

Profile of an Entrepreneurial Organization: Applied Urban Research Institute

The Applied Urban Research Institute (AURI) is a different kind of nonprofit. The agency operates best on the frontier of institutional wilderness, working with virtuous leaders and urban residents to promote planning and apply research to change communities.

"We don't exactly fit the mold for nonprofits," said Jim Scott, AURI's executive director since its inception in 1994. "There are organizations that see planning as something you do while you're waiting to solve the real problem. We see it in the reverse. We see a lot of money spent without a plan as what causes inefficiencies."

At AURI, the entrepreneurial spirit prevails. "We rely on unintended consequences. You have to set up the opportunity for those consequences," Scott said. "It's not chaos or a complete abandonment of reason.

"We are the kind of organization that requires people to be creatively involved. We have a competition of ideas that gets us to the best ideas. We are about ideas and committed to principles," Scott said.

"Social entrepreneurship is what nonprofits have been doing for a long time. We just now understand what it is," said Richard Ruiz of El Centro. "It allows us to accept certain things that were not acceptable in our world years ago—like earned income." "We need to bring creative products to the market that are affordable to the families we serve," Ruiz said. "We have the model that works. Now it is a matter of the entrepreneurial spirit and organizational capacity to handle the workload. The difference between the private sector and the nonprofit sector really boils down to they are driven by profits, while we are driven by our social mission. We want to generate revenues and earned income so we can reinvest back into the community to help families build assets and control their own destinies and major life choices. And that is the beauty of the nonprofit sector."

Questions for Funders

- Does the organization continually pursue opportunities that are aligned with its mission?

- Does the organization take the lead in identifying unmet community needs and developing innovative solutions to address those needs?

- Does the organization understand the importance of crossing boundaries, as appropriate, between the public, private, and nonprofit sectors?

- Does the organization invest resources in professional development for management, staff, and volunteers?

- Are leaders active in and do they hold leadership positions in other community or professional organizations at the local, state, and national levels?

Effective Nonprofits Are Adaptable

Adaptable organizations are able to respond quickly and with flexibility to changing circumstances in the environment in which they operate. Adaptable organizations are aware of both sudden and gradual changes in staff, clients, funding sources, legal requirements, and community needs and are able to make the adjustments necessary to respond adequately to such changes. These organizations are resilient and have the ability to rebound from setbacks and continue their pursuit of the mission.

An adaptable organization is expected to respond to changing circumstances. Its leadership does not use scarce resources, finances, or staff inefficiently by seeking unrealistic or inappropriate goals in a changing environment. An adaptable organization provides quality services to its clientele and current technologies to its staff. It is a learning organization that continually examines ways to operate efficiently and effectively.

Profile of an Adaptable Nonprofit: Heart of America Family Services

"If an organization gets to the point where it thinks 'we've got it, we're there,' that's when things are going to come unglued," said Betsy Vander Velde, president of Heart of America Family Services—where, in the past few years, the staff has tripled, programs have gone bilingual, a major revenue source disappeared overnight, and aggressive partnerships have moved more than three dozen agencies to work together to raise parent education and child care standards in every corner of greater Kansas City.

Fifteen years ago the organization ran a fledgling program to care for kids whose parents were working. When more parents went to work, the organization responded with new services, including a support program for kids who were home without supervision after school. The agency developed Homefront, a collaboration devoted to improving the quality of parent education, including sharing the latest research about early brain development. The organization has been part of a progressive partnership to increase the number of accredited child care centers in Kansas City and took the lead to develop a single phone line that connects parents to child care referrals across fifteen counties.

Responding to the needs of families moving from welfare to work, Heart of America Family Services placed child care resource and referral staff on site at the Missouri Department of Family Services. "We never stop doing community analysis and environmental scans. One reason we've been around for 120 years is our ability to respond effectively and quickly to the changing environments and stay very clearly focused on what we do best," said Vander Velde.

Questions for Funders

- Can the organization identify major changes it has made in the past several years to meet changing community needs?

- Can the organization analyze whether and how the changing environment can work to its advantage?

- Do continual innovation and learning prevail throughout the organization?

- Does the organization use partnerships, strategic alliances, and collaborations to leverage opportunities?

Effective Nonprofits Are Customer Focused

A customer-focused organization's primary concern is meeting the needs of its stakeholders, including the larger community as well as the direct recipients of its services. The organization understands which services customers value, how to develop new services that respond to customers' needs, and how to improve existing services. Customers know their needs are important to the organization and each is treated as a "market of one."

The staff of a customer-focused organization value and respect their constituents and treat them as they would want to be treated. Everything about the organization's physical surroundings expresses its regard for its customers. The areas that are seen and used by customers are as attractive and well maintained as the areas used by organization staff. Appointments and meetings are arranged for the convenience of the customers. Where possible and appropriate, customers and community members have well-established and formal avenues for voicing their concerns about the services provided.

Profile of a Customer-Focused Nonprofit: Swope Corridor Renaissance

The hard urban edges of Kansas City's Swope Corridor are softened when you know that more girls and boys live along the corridor than in any other place in the city. According to Census data, the twelve hundred school-age children crowding the one-square-mile area represent the city's highest density of children. The corridor has the greatest number of single mothers and the highest number of Temporary Assistance for Needy Families (TANF) block grant recipients. The area also tops the city's list for child abuse crimes.

In town hall meetings with residents, a summer program for children and an after-school program during the school year were identified as the neighborhood's primary needs. As the Swope Corridor Renaissance group considered the need to care for the community's children while their parents or guardians were working, the idea of creating an urban youth campus emerged with four churches. The Southeast Branch of the Kansas City Public Library joined the campus, and the W.E.B. DuBois Learning Center became the telecommunications and technology hub, linking the urban campus facilities, offering students hands-on training, and providing a way to trace students' progress.

Word of mouth has created a groundswell of support for the program. The initial program enrolled 93 children. In its third year, the program received 600 applications and was able to expand to 375 children. To make improvements, the group listens to feedback from all sides. Teachers send home questionnaires to keep communication channels open. The children are also quick to offer suggestions. "We learned very early on that basketball is not just for boys. It's for boys and girls," said Jerry McEvoy, who serves as treasurer of the Swope Corridor Renaissance and program director of the Upper Room at the St. Louis Church.

"We are still learning about our customer," said the group's president, Margaret J. May. "It's very difficult to bring the single mom forward. We want to get closer to the mother to make her a part of the process. If the mother doesn't acknowledge the child's development, it's much tougher on the child."

Questions for Funders

- Does everyone connected to the organization treat customers with respect and courtesy?

- Are there well-established, readily available, and clearly publicized channels through which the opinions and concerns of customers may be expressed?

- Is feedback from all customers solicited and responded to on an ongoing basis?

- Does the organization understand the needs of stakeholders and constituencies?

Conclusion

The link between grantmakers and nonprofits is essential and unbreakable. Not only are funders and their boards expecting non-profits to provide clear outcomes regarding programs, they have a growing interest in the organizational performance and capability of nonprofit leaders to deliver the services effectively. The identification of these key attributes of effective nonprofit organizations is essential to provide a framework to monitor and communicate how our investments are adding value to the improvement of outcomes for the clientele of every nonprofit.

Chapter Four

Better Results Through Supportive Engagement

Alexa Cortes Culwell, CEO,
Charles and Helen Schwab Foundation

Lisa Sobrato Sonsini, Founding President,
Sobrato Family Foundation

Sterling K. Speirn, President,
Peninsula Community Foundation

Two perceptions are commonplace in our nonprofit sector:

- *A foundation's money makes a level playing field with grantees impossible.*
- *Money equals control. As a result, the power dynamic dictates that the relationship be less than authentic.*

In fact, so widespread and deeply held are these beliefs that they have come to frame a paradigm that few believe can ever be shifted.

For funders, "organizational effectiveness" can be treated as just another grants category, like the arts or youth development, or it

---

Note: To download the full report on OCGI or find out more about our foundations, go to any of our Web sites:

Peninsula Community Foundation: www.pcf.org

Charles and Helen Schwab Foundation: www.schwabfoundation.org

Sobrato Family Foundation: www.sobrato.com/foundation/

can be seen as a new opportunity to build value together with non-profit leaders. It can be approached with a rather mechanistic, fix-it mentality focused on the deficits of the nonprofit, or it can be seen as a developmental opportunity for both funder and nonprofit alike. It can be relegated to consultants, intermediaries, and evaluators, or it can be seen as an opportunity for high engagement between funders and practitioners. It can be planned and organized around a highly detailed blueprint, or it can grow out of a commitment to learning and shared discovery. It can be launched with a competitive request for proposals process, or it can begin with an invitation and dialogue. It can be framed as a series of transactions, or it can be embedded in a web of relationships.

In this chapter, we discuss a choice our foundations made to think about "organizational effectiveness" work differently. We have found that making a conscious choice to create an environment where foundations and nonprofits can work together as peers and partners in a learning community allows funders to get better results on both grant investments and social goals.

In 1997, when our three foundations came together to explore how we could work together to address challenges facing the human services sector in our community, we were hardly aware of the alternatives. We did not think in these terms. While all three had track records in funding human service agencies in an overlapping geographic region (the Peninsula, crowned by San Francisco to the north and rooted in Silicon Valley to the south), our differences were pronounced. The Peninsula Community Foundation was a public charity with a thirty-four-year history and a seasoned professional staff. The Schwab Foundation was five years old and growing rapidly, with two professional staff but no previous experience in launching initiatives. The Sobrato Family Foundation was brand new and led by a family member.

However, our differences didn't prevent us from exploring possibilities in an open discussion, inspired by a *Harvard Business Review* article (Letts, Ryan, and Grossman, 1997) that challenged foundations to move beyond program funding and build organizational capacity. The article spelled out a fundamental truth that would become our mandate: "Foundations need to find ways to make grants that not only fund programs but also build up the organizational capabilities that nonprofit groups need for delivering and sustaining quality."

A few months later, the Organizational Capacity Grants Initiative (OCGI) was born. After much discussion and negotiation, we arrived at a value proposition for OCGI we could endorse unanimously:

- Sixteen nonprofits would each receive at least $100,000 in funding for capacity-building work.
- The foundations would learn new ways of thinking and acting.
- The foundations and nonprofits would learn together to work more effectively in the community.

This initial dialogue between a few foundations soon became a collaborative grantmaker and grantee partners working together with a total grants budget of $2 million and an additional $425,000 invested in supporting activities. Three years later, OCGI would conclude with noteworthy—and, in some cases, transformational—changes in organizational effectiveness for most of the nonprofits and all the foundations that participated.

Supportive Engagement: Aspirations and Realities

While the organizational outcomes were significant parts of OCGI, this chapter focuses on an innovative element that drove the success of the initiative, namely the creation of an environment where foundations and nonprofits could work together as peers and partners in a learning community. We came to describe this critical element as "supportive engagement."

The First Challenge: Collectively Designing the Initiative

Supportive engagement involved a triad of relationships:

- Among the three foundations
- Between the foundations and the nonprofits who agreed to participate
- Among the sixteen participating nonprofits

Supportive engagement certainly had its challenges. First, our foundations had to be willing to work together to fund and manage the initiative, giving each other an equal voice even though our financial contributions and philanthropic experience varied. In retrospect, it's clear that the early dynamic we established for the interrelationships among the foundations set a powerful example and modeled key values that framed and supported the initiative.

Working on its own, an independent foundation is in a relatively simple world; it can see itself as the hub of a wheel with spokes radiating out to each grantee at the rim. The hub, at the center, has only one voice and one set of values, and enjoys the orderliness of spokes connecting and organizing the nonprofits for the benefit of the foundation.

In contrast, OCGI began with a huddle instead of a hub. We started with three foundations, and soon added two more partners—CompassPoint, a management support organization for nonprofits, and BTW Consultants, a firm specializing in planning and evaluation. Now there were five voices, with diverse experiences and insights, and no one of us was "in control."

We had just enough shared values, trust, and tolerance for ambiguity to move the idea of the initiative to the next stage. Even in the early design phase, we had already established a culture of exploration and dialogue among a peer group of foundation leaders and expert consultants.

The Second Challenge: Getting Buy-In from Nonprofit Partners

We invited sixteen human service organizations to participate in the initiative as equal players. It's not hard to imagine the skepticism and doubts many of them brought to the table the first time we convened the group. Rather than announcing what we intended to do *to* them or *for* them, we explained that we wanted to do something *with* them—something we had yet to fully figure out. Though the cynics might have moved closer to the door, the good will of the foundations and our reputations for honesty earned us the opportunity to make our case.

We observed that as foundations that primarily fund locally, we were joined at the hip with our local human service organizations. Their strengths and weaknesses ultimately determined the quantity and quality of services provided to our community. They, not we, were experts in domestic violence, homelessness, after-school programs, volunteerism, and family support services. We were offering them flexible funds for capacity building, but we weren't going to be the hub—and they couldn't simply behave like good spokes. We weren't trying to build a wheel but a stronger nonprofit engine to navigate challenging terrain, and we didn't have a detailed blueprint to follow.

In exchange for specific financial and technical support for each nonprofit's plan to improve organizational effectiveness, we explained, they would have to commit to participating fully in a learning cohort. They had to be willing to join the foundation leaders in cohort gatherings and plan and help design the initiative throughout its three-year span. Within the paradigm of intractable inequality between grantmakers and grantees, we were essentially demoting ourselves while promoting the nonprofit leaders. We believed that each participant brought a unique viewpoint and expertise to the table, and we hoped we might discover how this whole might exceed the sum of its disparate parts. We wanted to transform our work to better serve the community, and our instincts told us this was better done as a supportive community rather than in isolation.

Some of the veteran executive directors, protective of their limited time, were skeptical of the value they would derive from the cohort meetings. They might have thought the transaction-based approach of grant proposal, funding, and reporting on outcomes would do just fine, a kind of "OCGI-lite" for busy nonprofit executives. It was certainly a reasonable request, much more realistic given the pressures on everyone's daily schedules. But it would not create or engender supportive engagement. OCGI was about more than money and individual organization work. It was about strengthening all the partners through collective action, specifically, committing to simple acts such as sharing, reflecting, and learning together.

Something happened at our first meeting with the nonprofits that set the tone for the success of the learning community. We outlined our preliminary design for the initiative with the nonprofits and announced the funding would be $30,000 per organization per year for three years. The amount had been determined through discussion among the foundations and was based on two issues. The first was a guesstimate of how much our boards would be willing to allocate; the second was our judgment call on an amount that would make a difference in a human service organization, where funds for capacity building were often mere fantasy.

As the large group broke into smaller groups to discuss the design, grumblings about the funding level were heard. It became clear that the nonprofits thought $30,000 a year for three years did not justify the commitment. There was a momentary silence, and the facilitator asked the group to discuss what amount would justify the commitment and why. In the end, the executives advocated for $50,000 per year for two years. The foundation leaders took a deep breath and agreed. We had released the spokes.

The Third Challenge: Strengthening Relationships

The third challenge of supportive engagement was the deepening of nonprofit-to-nonprofit relationships and synergies. Some of the nonprofit executives knew each other quite well, while others had never met or were only glancing acquaintances. Some were seasoned veterans, while others were relatively new on the job. All the practitioners worked in geographically overlapping or contiguous communities, but their missions varied widely—from at-risk youth activities and enrichment to job training for people with disabilities, volunteer recruitment, and conflict resolution, to name just a few.

Unwittingly, this "Noah's Ark" aspect enabled the executives to come to the table with none of the competition that might accompany a more homogeneous peer group. The executive directors told us they didn't worry about the subtle or not-so-subtle comparisons foundations naturally make among organizations providing similar services. This diversity proved to be a benefit for building relationships but also a challenge for the initiative as we sought to find common ground and relevance for the disparate organizations.

It was not clear precisely how the nonprofit leaders would use the potential resources of the cohort. The foundations had explicitly avoided any mention or requirement of collaboration among the practitioners. We were familiar with the resentment nonprofit leaders experience when foundations arbitrarily or artificially impose the expectation that organizations should collaborate. Under such circumstances, collaboration has been called "an unnatural act by non-consenting adults." In this case, we could only assert that the cohort gatherings would be organized to support the work of the initiative.

In the end, the projects funded by the grants clustered in four areas:

- Technology
- Marketing and fund development
- Human resources
- Leadership, management, and governance

Eleven of the sixteen organizations received funding for technology-related projects.

And so the learning table was set. Attendance was mandatory. No one was sure whether it would be a catered affair or a soup kitchen, a brown-bag lunch or a grand potluck. The only thing that was certain was that there would be much learning along the way.

Lesson 1: Trust Is the Ultimate Operating Principle

Once we agreed to work together as foundations, consultants, and nonprofit leaders, we needed to declare the operating principles that would guide the development of each component of the initiative.

Broadly speaking, trust is critical for any partnership to work, and it takes time to build, even in the nonprofit sector where our work is all about social good. It is important not to take trust for granted. A group needs to carefully address it from the moment planning begins. In our case, many of the participating foundations and nonprofits in our initiative were strangers to one another, with little basis for trust.

So our first principle was trust. After spending time conceptualizing the initiative, the foundations now trusted one another, but would we trust the nonprofits, and would the nonprofits trust us, let alone trust one another? And how do you build trust?

Justifying the Risk

We began with two strategies. The first was to ask the practitioners whether this deal was worth the risk. In traditional program- or project-based funding, the scope of inquiry between grantmaker and grantee is usually limited to the outcomes stated in the grant proposal. How did the tutoring program go? What were the outcomes of the free medical clinic? In OCGI, the focus would be on building organizational capacity, and that could lead to scrutiny of almost any aspect of an organization's operations—governance, bookkeeping, fundraising, management, or strategic planning. As we got to know the nonprofits, they ran the risk of having their weaknesses and problems exposed. Then, as conventional wisdom would have it, the foundations might pronounce them deficient and withdraw funding.

Indeed, in almost every discussion about a grantmaker's role in capacity building, this is usually the first objection that surfaces. The implication is that grantmakers are not to be trusted with the truth. We want only good news. We are the punitive perfectionists and to trust us is to commit organizational suicide.

It was time for the foundations to come clean. We confessed that we routinely faced the very same organizational challenges as our nonprofit colleagues. We had less-than-perfect boards and staffs. Our own leadership and management skills were under-developed. The industry we worked in was in a time of great change and instability. Our strategic plans needed reworking. Peninsula Community Foundation had even applied for its own capacity-building grant. The Schwab Foundation was embarking on a planning process to improve its capacity and performance. The Sobrato Family Foundation was struggling to enhance its operational capacity by hiring staff for the first time. "Welcome to the group," said one executive director.

It was important to acknowledge that we were all striving to improve the complex, imperfect organizations we lead. It meant there could be no double standard in the cohort. The foundations would not play the Wizard of Oz, bestowing brains, hearts, or courage while hiding behind a screen to mask our own imperfections. It was an important moment of solidarity, and it built trust.

Walking the Talk

The second strategy was to practice what we preached from the outset. Each nonprofit was expected to identify its own organizational priorities and determine how grant funds would be spent.

OCGI did not specify capacity-building categories that would be eligible for funding. Rather, the initiative's learning emphasis required that each organization undertake a planning and prioritizing process through which it identified its organizational needs. "Trust the agencies" became a mantra for the foundations as we sought to bring life to a new vision for working with our nonprofit partners.

The foundations were essentially giving up control—but not responsibility or our commitment and role in contributing to a successful outcome. We were taking a leap of faith that the nonprofits would consider and discuss our ideas, feedback, and guidance in the spirit of improving results. We were adopting a new way of thinking, and establishing trust in the process.

The best example of thinking and acting in new ways occurred early on. After completing internal assessments and updating strategic plans as necessary, the sixteen organizations submitted case statements outlining their proposed capacity-building projects. The foundations and consultants met with each organization to discuss them. On first review, we were disappointed by many of the proposals. They seemed like deferred maintenance rather than the highly strategic projects we had envisioned for the initiative. Proposals for telephone systems, branding projects, and computers seemed short-sighted. How would these projects improve effectiveness?

Despite these concerns about the proposals, the foundations decided the nonprofits needed to make the final decision on how they would apply the funding. In most cases, as it turned out, the projects that initially appeared to be deferred maintenance were indeed transformational.

But what about the proposals we really struggled to justify? Two executives stuck to their original proposals despite significant concern from the foundations. In one instance, unfortunately, the final evaluation report showed little overall improvement for the nonprofit. But, for another, the outcomes were powerful. The director proposed funding for a new operations position that would allow her to spend more time building her board and preparing them for a capital campaign. She exceeded her own expectations, as well as ours. The successful campaign enabled her to expand her facility and increase the number of children served.

In another instance, an executive director who had submitted a case for technology funding changed her proposal completely when the Schwab Foundation shared its experience in implementing a new technology system. After hearing the difficulties inherent in that undertaking, the director realized the complexity was more than the organization was prepared to handle and picked a project more poised for success. She would eventually introduce a new technology system with other funding, but only after addressing other critical areas first.

Thinking and acting in new ways enabled us to relinquish control of grant dollar allocations to the nonprofits. While some projects did not perform as well as we had hoped, the success stories outweighed the few failures. More important, we learned that the failures yielded important lessons and were worth the risk when trust was at stake.

Questions for Funders

- Do we work to instill a sense of trust with our nonprofit partners?
- Are we open about our own challenges and weaknesses?
- If we encourage nonprofits to admit their failures, are we prepared to help them overcome challenges rather than hold their weaknesses against them?

Lesson 2: Supportive Engagement Requires Learning, Reflection, Inclusiveness, and Transparency

Trusting one another to work together in a spirit of success and mutual support was the keystone upon which the other operating principles could rest. Following trust were learning, reflection, inclusiveness, and transparency. These were critical to the initiative because we were forging a new experiment that required ongoing assessment. "Sticking to our plan," especially given that none of us had done this before, would have been a disaster. Learning by doing and taking time to reflect allowed us to adjust course as necessary so that we could achieve the best outcomes. Setting up a process that was inclusive allowed us to hear many voices and ensure greater participation, which was one of the distinguishing elements of supportive engagement. Finally, transparency allowed us to see the real issues so that we could forge solutions with a chance of success.

Learning

Participants—both nonprofits and foundations—were expected to share the challenges and successes they encountered while building capacity within their organizations. In designing the initiative, we employed the term *cohort* to convey the collective experience of the participants as they created the OCGI learning community.

Foundations were partners at the "learning table"—not only advising in areas of expertise but sharing their own organizational challenges and using the initiative and the expertise of practitioners as a means for their own growth and development.

Reflection

OCGI intentionally provided a time and a place for reflection; it was a required element of participation in the initiative. The practice of reflection was structured into virtually all activities.

Specifically, this meant time in every agenda to reflect on the challenges of implementing the plans made possible by grant dollars as well as larger organizational issues that emerged as a result. Consequently, OCGI engendered a shift from *reactive* to *reflective* practice within and among all participants.

Inclusiveness

The initiative launched with a process that was as inclusive as possible. When our foundations agreed to partner, we immediately began co-creating the initiative, enlisting third-party consultants to form a steering committee to help craft and facilitate the initiative and conduct the evaluation. As the human service organizations came on board, we began to experiment with their participation and sought to involve them meaningfully in the design and implementation without overtaxing their time. Accordingly, as the initiative emerged, everyone had a stake in the design.

Transparency

Linked to the value of inclusiveness was our commitment to transparency, which was a deterrent to lapsing into more conventional foundation roles. For example, when the foundations and nonprofits met to discuss the proposals for allocating funding, one foundation leader suggested we share all the proposals with all the nonprofits so they might benefit from one another's work. Not to do so would mean we were again sitting at the hub with all the information and dealing individually with each organization as a spoke. After an animated discussion about the appropriateness of such an unconventional approach, we realized we needed the permission of all the executive directors to share their proposals. In quick order, they all gave their consent, and the shroud of secrecy that overlaid the traditional grantmaker-grantee relationship was lifted.

Discussion of our governance practices became another interesting example of transparency, especially among the foundation colleagues. The behind-the-scenes dynamics of boards of directors are seldom discussed inside a nonprofit or foundation, let alone externally. We had promised the organizations a minimum of two years' funding, but none of us had received multiyear commitments from our boards. As foundation leaders, we openly discussed the challenges of convincing our boards of the fruitfulness of the initiative. We often brainstormed what kind of evidence each foundation required, supporting one another toward success and opening up a rich dialogue about the decision-making dynamics of our boards.

Ultimately, with one another's help and support, the foundations raised the funds needed and even added a third year to the initiative. More important, we extended our learning to the larger group. After each board meeting, we shared our stories with the entire cohort.

Questions for Funders

- How do we and our grantees learn from one another to encourage growth and development?
- Is our decision-making process transparent to our grantees?
- How do we involve nonprofits in our grant designs and implementation?

Lesson 3: Successful Partnerships Contain Common Elements

Supportive engagement was a vital element in helping nonprofits achieve organizational effectiveness, but it alone could not have produced the significant results of OCGI. In the end, four additional elements emerged as critical components of the initiative's design and the ingredients for success. As the authors of other chapters have discussed, the definition of *effectiveness* depends on the organization. In OCGI, we found our relationships required slightly different approaches with each organization. However, just as the authors of other chapters have found common traits to effective organizations, we discovered common elements to successful partnerships:

- Grant dollars for capacity-building projects
- Supportive engagement
- Active reflection
- Leadership

First, discrete *grant dollars* targeted specific capacity-building projects within the nonprofits—$100,000 over two years in extremely flexible funding and an additional $25,000 for the third year. This is probably how many foundations initially conceptualize grantmaking for capacity building. For us, it was only the first resource committed to the project.

As the initiative evolved, we came to realize that the capacity-building money, and the work it catalyzed, was only a part of the organizations' success. It must be supported by the discipline of *supportive engagement* and the practice of *active reflection* to enable higher achievement. Together, these two elements created a web of relationships and learning opportunities and established a context and a place for leaders—who too often work in isolation—to receive and give support among peers.

OCGI was premised on the belief that the financial transaction was no more important than the discussion that led to and followed it. According to one key informant, "It was almost like the grant was our excuse to meet, and then in our meeting we learned so much."

The fourth element, *leadership*—among the nonprofit executive directors, their senior staffs, and their boards—was the final critical ingredient. Strong leadership created a multiplier effect, enabling organizations to leverage the resources of the core elements and create a new trajectory toward long-term and sustainable transformation.

Questions for Funders

- What opportunities do our nonprofit partners have to work with colleagues from peer organizations and to reflect upon their work for higher achievement?

- How do we support strong leadership in our nonprofit partners?

- How can we best provide our nonprofit partners with the grant dollars they need for capacity-building projects?

Lesson 4: Strong Relationships Are Essential for Successful Supportive Engagement

Like explorers of old, we set out on a voyage of discovery without a detailed map. It was an ambitious endeavor with an unprecedented joint command structure, and one that would succeed or fail based upon the shared strengths of the entire party. The power and efficacy of the new relationships we built were critical components for those organizations seeking to find the shores of organizational effectiveness. Many of our lessons learned are embedded in the stories shared in this chapter.

Ultimately, OCGI was a multifaceted partnership that worked because of the relationships that were forged. This is why supportive engagement matters in any foundation-nonprofit relationship. When relationships are nurtured, trust develops. Trust results in access to higher-quality information. Quality information encourages more meaningful dialogue about what is possible. Dialogue allows the best solutions to emerge and be funded.

Here are some additional reflections on our experiences with supportive engagement.

The Foundation-to-Foundation Relationship

As is true with most partnerships, collaboration with colleague foundations depends heavily on interpersonal relationships, learning styles, and shared values. Availability and curiosity were critical from the beginning. Making time to explore ideas with each other, to support an ongoing dialogue and intellectual quest, was essential. Believing we had something to learn from our peers, and something for them to learn from us, gave us the benefit of multiple viewpoints, opinions, and hunches that sometimes led to inspiration and at other times encouraged us in the face of exasperation and doubt. Trust and a commitment to honest inquiry got us through the anxious moments when some partners' tolerance for ambiguity and uncertainty were put to the test. The group dynamic enabled us to stay the course because it wasn't just one executive director or one foundation making the investment. It was collective action. The temptation to give up is only natural in this sort of effort, but different people have different triggers; when one or another was tempted to give up, the dynamic of the group provided encouragement to stick with the initiative.

Money needs to be secondary. The value of each partner's contribution cannot be measured by the level of its funding. In fact, each foundation made significant but different levels of funding to the initiative. This was further demonstrated by our consultants, CompassPoint and BTW, who contributed expertise in facilitation, initiative design, and evaluation. Senior leaders from these organizations joined us as peers and early co-creators. They brought no money to the table, but they contributed a wealth of experience and the same curiosity and passion for the sector we have. Our consultants have their own stories of how the work of OCGI transformed their thinking about their work with nonprofits.

OCGI's collaboration among foundations pushed us out of our comfort zones so that we could transform our thinking and challenge old assumptions. Coming together as equal partners required long discussion of key elements of the initiative in order to make decisions. Each discussion revealed unique perspectives, experiences, and values. As a result we grew as leaders, both personally and professionally. Our work in the communities we serve was transformed for the better. As a result of OCGI, the foundations experienced marked improvements in our own approaches to our work.

The Sobrato Family Foundation has taken the experience of OCGI and aligned much of its grantmaking around the initiative's core values. For example, almost all its grants are now made for capacity building, even deferred maintenance. It is building stronger individual relationships with fewer nonprofits but offering larger grants. And it has completely overhauled its grant application process to eliminate lengthy proposals, focusing instead on face-to-face meetings with each applicant to jointly explore and identify the organization's greatest need.

The Charles and Helen Schwab Foundation is co-creating all its initiatives in tandem with nonprofit partners. One cohort of substance abuse treatment providers is called the BEST (Building Effective Substance Abuse Treatment) Initiative. Forming a cohort around a common mission area has had several advantages. For example, organization leaders in the cohort can more readily exchange lessons learned that are immediately relevant to peers. Applying lessons learned across organizations participating in OCGI was often more like comparing apples to oranges. In addition, evaluation is easier with BEST because evaluators can assess programs with similar missions and services or cluster groups that are working on similar capacity areas.

The Peninsula Community Foundation has also launched an Environmental Solutions Forum, a cohort of twelve nonprofit environmental education groups and two county offices of education. Although partners in this cohort are all in the same field, there is tremendous variety in size and scope of operations among participating organizations, so many of the same challenges apply. An added benefit of forming a cohort within a specific field is that there are more early opportunities for collaboration among cohort partners.

The three authors of this chapter continue to talk and meet regularly. We are even working on several new projects together. Interestingly, we have each been elected board members of our regional association of grantmakers, an ideal podium for discussing the importance of partnership in our sector.

Grantmakers and Nonprofits

A unique aspect of OCGI was the involvement of multiple foundations and multiple organizations. The presence of multiple foundations enhanced our ability to challenge the paradigm of inequality between grantmakers and grantees. When practitioners saw the foundations disagree or express alternative viewpoints, they were encouraged to do the same. When they saw that we didn't have a grand design or a secret strategy, they realized they would have to be equal contributors if the initiative was to have value for them. This reinforced the notion that we were all leaders and peers with a common agenda for our community.

Pursuing the common goal of organizational effectiveness was a great leveler. Stressing our commonalities as leaders with similar challenges in governance and management, fundraising, and allocation of scarce resources invited full participation at the learning table. It enabled us to co-create the initiative in partnership, with foundation and nonprofit leaders forming committees to review critical design issues, plan cohort meetings, and determine agendas for our annual retreats. Everyone had the chance to lead group discussions and to be a featured speaker in areas of expertise.

Still, we discovered there was no way to accelerate the establishment of trust. Proclaiming equality didn't make it so. It took time before the chemistry of the cohort really started to gel. By then, the regularity of the cohort gatherings had established a routine and familiarity that had increasing utility for the nonprofits, who were tackling ambitious change agendas within their organizations.

Likewise, the foundations had come to rely increasingly on the nonprofit executive directors for guidance and support. For example, the Schwab Foundation borrowed some of the newly designed human resource practices from one organization, thereby putting to use the very systems the OCGI funding helped create.

We sought one another's guidance and wisdom on the challenges of leadership we shared. Schwab Foundation CEO Alexa Culwell remembers a one-on-one conversation with a nonprofit director: "I knew she was struggling with overcoming staff resistance to new strategic plans, and I was in the same boat. We shared our experiences, which was enormously comforting and helped me stay the course."

Informal encounters proved in some ways as valuable as the scheduled cohort meetings. Each foundation invited groups of three or four practitioners to meet for no-agenda lunches. We talked shop; we talked projects; we just talked. We also encouraged nonprofit executives to meet in their own small groups without the foundations, and we offered to pick up the lunch tab for these encounters.

At our one-year anniversary, the foundations and nonprofits gathered for a day-long retreat to take stock. As we went around the circle, all the participants shared what the OCGI experience had meant to them. Honesty, earnestness, and special camaraderie now filled the room. We had barely begun the hard work of building capacity, but on that day we knew we had become peers and that we were witnessing something important—the phenomenon we would eventually call supportive engagement. Simply stated, each leader at the table was supporting the others to do a better job in their organizations and in the community.

Like anything of value, supportive engagement came at a price. High engagement takes a tremendous amount of time. We certainly understand the efficiency of delegating the responsibilities of implementation to staff or consultants. This is a prevalent model in the funding world. First, foundation CEOs and program officers commission extensive studies and literature reviews. They design elaborate strategies, complete with time lines, outcome statements, and, more recently, explicit theories of change. Their boards approve funding, and then execution is left to consultants, evaluators, and report writers.

In contrast, three foundation CEOs and their vice presidents or program officers were frontline participants throughout the three-year OCGI initiative. Senior executives from the consulting partners did likewise. All the nonprofits were represented by their executive directors. Recently, a foundation colleague challenged us to justify the time it took to manage the OCGI web of relationships.

We replied earnestly, "How do we *not* justify it?!" Implicit in this response is our shared value that partnership is critical to advance the social issues and causes we feel so strongly about. None of us alone can achieve the ambitious social agendas we have adopted.

Supportive engagement created trusting relationships that yielded better outcomes. It's difficult to be successful at any endeavor when you don't have all the information you need. Often, the traditional processes for transacting grants are not the right vehicles for understanding the full story of the challenges and obstacles an organization faces. Written grant applications and formal site visits tend to encourage only the most optimistic assessments. But well-tended one-on-one relationships, formed around common goals, bring about a level of trust and candor that is golden. A grantmaker who has all the information can clearly identify priorities and bring the right resources to bear, optimizing the potential for success.

The experience of OCGI inspired one organization to treat other foundations differently. The executive director shared this story: "After participating in OCGI, we now approach our relationships with foundations in a more proactive way that has yielded significant benefits. When we recently received a new grant, we invited the foundation to come visit our organization in order to get to know us better. While this site visit was outside the foundation's standard protocol, they agreed to it. This initiated an ongoing, in-depth relationship in which we share our successes but also the challenges we face. Because this foundation understands who we are and what we do, they have exposed us to other foundations. We have actually been able to short-circuit the funding process with some new foundations because of their strong recommendation." Building a strong foundation relationship, in this case, not only enhanced the first relationship but also forged the way for new partnerships with other foundations.

From the grantmaker's perspective, the richness of the grantmaker-nonprofit relationship highlighted the built-in limitations of grantmaking based only on due diligence. Alexa Culwell described a professional ennui that comes with merely writing grant checks: "Looking back, when I thought my purpose was to read sterile proposals, go on scripted site visits, and respond with template decline or approval letters, I was bored. Now I'm not." Sobrato Family Foundation president Lisa Sonsini made a similar observation: "Instead of transacting grants, OCGI allowed us to engage in the life of the nonprofits. The work became challenging and fulfilling, and the relationships led to deeper partnership and better outcomes."

Nonprofit-to-Nonprofit Relationships

As foundation officers, we are probably least qualified to report on this aspect of OCGI. Our hope had been that the practitioners, while not formally collaborating on a joint project, would come to be a peer-support and peer-mentoring resource for one another. We provided a variety of trainers and consultants for outside expertise, but we always believed that the experience of the nonprofit leaders could be converted into a more accessible resource for mutual support.

More than half the nonprofits indicated in their final reports that the "high-quality relationships" they developed with other organizations and their leaders may represent the "greatest legacy of OCGI." Not only did the quality of relationships improve, but the breadth of connections broadened. Despite their different services and programs, they reported they had "more in common with each other" than they initially thought. One executive director said, "I believe I have found a community that will transcend OCGI."

A more tangible benefit was the way in which the nonprofits shared information and resources with one another. OCGI participants reported that they looked to one another for support in a variety of ways—by sharing experiences, reports, and instruments, and, in some cases, even consultants. New strategic partnerships among various participants developed. Three organizations tackled a common capacity-building project, sharing consultants and negotiating vendor contracts together. Other organizations developed partnerships to complement services and decrease service duplication. A child care organization began providing its services for two organizations that had not previously considered such a collaboration. The cohort practitioners decided on their own to create a council of nonprofits for one county. In the ultimate act of collaboration, two nonprofits merged on the basis of the relationships forged between the two executives during the initiative.

It's a testimony to the strong relationships that developed through OCGI, and to the integrity of the work, that toward the end of year two the foundations explored adding a third year to the initiative. We wanted to continue learning alongside the nonprofits and wondered if a smaller grant of $25,000 would keep the nonprofit leaders coming to the table. It did—everyone returned for a third year, confirming that the value of the initiative went far beyond money.

To sunset the initiative after two years would have been to squander the resources the nonprofit leaders were developing among and for themselves. Much like the value of social capital among neighbors, we came to see the value of these relationships as a kind of "sector capital" that would be a resource these leaders could draw upon for years to come. We collectively determined the additional third year of funding would focus on leadership development for the nonprofit executives and senior staff.

Questions for Funders

- How do we work to strengthen our relationships with nonprofits? With other funders?
- What can we do to encourage our nonprofit partners to work more closely with one another?

Conclusion

OCGI was an initiative committed to helping foundations and nonprofits generate greater results for the communities they serve. In the search for enhanced effectiveness, for both ourselves and the nonprofits, we experimented with almost every aspect of the grant-making process and challenged some of our basic assumptions. We documented every aspect of the experiment and tried to capture the outcomes of OCGI for each participant, understanding that the story was only worth telling if it yielded strong results. The full story is captured in an evaluation report by BTW Consultants, *Building Effective Organizations: An Evaluation of the Organizational Capacity Grants Initiative*, and is available on our Web sites, listed at the beginning of the chapter. We invite your comments and inquiries.

From the Organizational Capacity Grants Initiative, we learned that supportive engagement is a critical element for achieving organizational effectiveness. While the emphasis on relationships was by no means the only critical element of OCGI's success, we believe it challenged so many of our common assumptions and practices that it was worthy of exploration. Yet it's not easy to describe how relationships are forged because they are by their very nature difficult to capture in a practical way.

OCGI taught us that nurturing strong, trusting relationships around a common goal optimizes success in achieving our social missions, provides a more meaningful experience in the process, and creates more sustainable community assets for future collaborations. This key investment of time for relationships was the main driver of OCGI and therefore makes our lessons applicable to a wide array of foundations. The initiative could have easily been "bigger" or "smaller" by simply including more, or fewer, nonprofit agencies or recruiting other foundations to provide more financial support. Instead the main lesson of the initiative was about substance and style—how we did the work. And the "how" of the work required an investment of time. For example, the Sobrato Family Foundation provided as much time and energy to the process as the other foundations did, even though it is a smaller operation with only one staff person.

Our foundations began the OCGI experiment with many notions and rationales about why it might be impossible to truly collaborate with our nonprofit colleagues. We completed the experiment convinced that there is great potential for our sector if we learn to work together in new ways.

Chapter Five

Cultivating a Culture of Measurement

Melinda T. Tuan, Co-Founder,
The Roberts Enterprise Development Fund

The philanthropic sector is constantly in search of reliable information about nonprofit organizations and the impact of their work. In this era of shrinking assets, limited funds, and increased pressure to demonstrate fiscal responsibility, grantmakers in particular are looking for ways to identify strong organizations, measure outcomes, and ensure they make sound investments.

In recent years, funders have placed greater emphasis on financial accountability and social outcome measurement for the nonprofit programs they fund. Grantmakers are demanding that nonprofit organizations measure their individual impacts and those of the entire nonprofit sector. The rapid growth of GuideStar.com, the creation of the United Way's Outcome Measurement Resource Network, the application of the Balanced Scorecard to nonprofit organizations, and the conversations about calculating a nonprofit's social return on investment (SROI) in the last decade are just a few examples.

Despite various efforts to strengthen the nonprofit sector's ability to report on performance, the truth is most foundations provide little funding or support to build organizations' capacity for financial reporting and the measurement of social outcomes. The philanthropic sector has historically not invested in nonprofit infrastructure and prefers to invest in programs. Additionally, most efforts to promote accountability and measurement are driven and demanded by funders or intermediaries, not by the nonprofits themselves.

Nonprofit organizations, to the surprise and chagrin of many grantmaking staff, are having difficulty producing timely and accurate financial and social outcome reports as required by their funders. It turns out that fulfilling what may seem like a clear and simple request for a report on a program grant can often cost more in time and resources than the value of the funds received for the actual program. The data reported out are only as good as the data entered in, and only as good as the organization has the capacity to produce, given its staff, technology, and other infrastructure. As a result, the funding community is increasingly frustrated and impatient about the low quality of reports received, and nonprofit organizations are struggling to explain their inability to meet the demands for greater accountability.

Certainly one solution is for grantmakers to provide more funding, not less, to build the capacity of nonprofit organizations for measuring both financial and social outcome results. Without a fundamental commitment from the philanthropic sector to build the organizational capacity of individual nonprofit organizations, no significant changes in reporting and accountability will occur. However, in the end, we as funders can demand as much information as we like and even invest heavily in nonprofit organizations' capacity to collect and report on data, but nothing will change unless individual nonprofit organizations embrace a culture of measurement. Nonprofit organizations must want the accountability of timely and accurate financial and social outcome information for themselves, to inform their own practice; only then will the grantmakers that fund them have a chance of receiving consistent and reliable reports.

In Search of an Information Oasis

Since 1997, we at The Roberts Enterprise Development Fund (REDF) have been investing in the capacity of our portfolio of nonprofit organizations to measure financial and social outcomes. Our search for an information oasis—a place where our knowledge needs and those of our grantees come together—had a dual purpose:

to find out whether nonprofits could successfully own and operate financially sustainable enterprises, and to find out whether employment in social purpose enterprises could result in lasting, positive changes in the lives of homeless and low-income individuals.

From the beginning, we theorized that nonprofit-run social purpose enterprises could be effective vehicles for achieving the double bottom line of making profits and helping people.

From our research, we have found that nonprofits can indeed run successful small businesses with a social mission, and the disadvantaged individuals employed in these businesses have experienced positive, lasting change in their lives. The financial and social outcomes we have collected are invaluable to us as funders, to the organizations we fund, and to the field of social purpose enterprise.

While searching for our own information oasis, we discovered in retrospect that we had helped cultivate a culture of measurement within most of our portfolio organizations and within REDF itself. Over time, our nonprofit partners had instilled a discipline of informed decision making by integrating financial and social outcome measurement into their daily activities. They had embraced the use of data to inform practice—resulting in a cultural change throughout their organizations over time—not just at the end of a project as an afterthought. While working with our nonprofit partners to measure their financial and social outcomes, we made many mistakes and learned a lot of important and hard lessons along the way, including the following:

- A foundation can best cultivate a culture of measurement within the nonprofits it funds by cultivating a culture of measurement within itself.
- Cultivating a culture of measurement takes time—more than you might think.
- Cultivating a culture of measurement takes significant resources, appropriate incentives, and lots of coordination.
- Organizations need to be ready for change.

- Technology is not the (entire) answer.
- Beware the slippery slope of evaluation—resist turning evaluation into a punitive system.
- Data only make a difference if they are used.

This chapter describes REDF's search for an information oasis and the effect the search had on our nonprofit partners. We acknowledge that our experience may not be typical when it comes to building measurement capacity, because we focus only on nonprofits that run businesses—which may already be a process of self-selection of organizations that have a penchant for measurement. In addition, we hire staff specifically for their background and skills in capacity building, and we expect them to work with our portfolio members over the long term. In some cases, we have partnered with portfolio members for over a decade and plan to continue investing in them for the foreseeable future.

So we do not expect that everyone will replicate what we and our nonprofit partners have done. However, in conversations with colleagues in the field, we have found our experience resonates with others' and we hope this case history and the lessons we learned will prove valuable to other funders and the overall nonprofit sector.

A Measurement Mirage

One of the toughest questions for both nonprofits and funders to answer is, How do you know your work really makes a difference? It is always difficult to measure results and have confidence that the findings are accurate and meaningful enough to inform better practice. Without timely, accurate outcome information about our work, we are all, nonprofits and foundations alike, laboring toward what may really be a mirage.

REDF began its work with nonprofits under the Homeless Economic Development Fund (HEDF) in the early 1990s. From the beginning, we were determined to collect information that would demonstrate the impact of our work. When we started, we asked the groups we funded if they could and would collect social outcome information on the homeless and low-income people they employed through their enterprises. When they all responded in the affirmative, we took their answers at face value. In 1996 we decided to publish a report to highlight the social and financial outcomes of our six-year, $6 million investment. We were interested in obtaining financial performance data on the enterprises as well as social outcome data on the enterprise employees to demonstrate the impact of this somewhat experimental approach to economic development.

We knew from working with the nonprofit-run enterprises that they had difficulty producing accurate and timely financial statements. This was not surprising given that most nonprofit accounting systems are designed for fund accounting, not business accounting. Additionally, many of the organizations had neither run a business before nor had staff with business backgrounds.

What did surprise us was that the nonprofits had equal, if not greater, difficulty reporting on the social outcomes of their enterprises. We hired an evaluator to gather social impact information from each funded organization. The evaluator found little reliable data on outputs (such as number of enterprise employees), let alone the outcomes in those people's lives. Through this process, we learned several key lessons:

- Nonprofits may promise more than they can deliver because they want to please a funder.
- Nonprofits may have the desire but not the capacity to measure financial and social outcomes.
- Funders need to invest in nonprofit organizational capacity to measure outcomes.
- Funders need to invest in their own organizational capacity to measure outcomes.

These lessons learned back in 1996 may seem rather basic now, but they came as a shock then. It was certainly hard to report our lack of financial or social outcome data to our donor at the time.

The Desert of Evaluation

Another lesson we learned was that *evaluation* is at best an unhelpful term. Most evaluation efforts do not provide helpful information to nonprofit organizations. To most nonprofits, an "evaluation" usually means a funder-imposed, retrospective, punitive measurement of performance that does not inform practice. Later, a number of our grantees confessed they made up some of the numbers the evaluator collected because they feared losing their HEDF funding.

Under these circumstances, both the nonprofit and the foundation lose, not to mention the people served by the nonprofit. As one of our grantees explained, "In the HEDF days, it was about reporting requirements—it didn't make our organization more effective, and it didn't further the [funding] relationship." It is difficult to encourage nonprofits to honestly assess the impact and value of their efforts when they feel only a positive outcome will get them another grant.

Preparing for the Search: Building Our Own Capacity for Measurement

Funders also need to ask the question, How do we know if our work makes a difference? To answer, we need to build the capacity of portfolio members to measure their own results. We also need to build our own capacity as funders to measure results. We need to be true to our own principles if we want to bring about lasting change in nonprofit measurement capacity; we need to model what we want our nonprofit partners to do.

In 1997, based on our experiences with HEDF, we adopted our current name and launched a new initiative to focus on a portfolio of ten nonprofit organizations running social purpose enterprises. Partnership, collaboration, and a mutual commitment to accountability and measurement were to be cornerstones of our approach. As we prepared for our next phase of funding, we purposefully changed our language to talk with nonprofits about "assessments" as opposed to "evaluations." We designed our initiative as a high-engagement funding relationship, where we at REDF wanted to know about and be involved in addressing both positive and negative issues within each organization and enterprise.

We increased our own organizational capacity, moving from a solo staff member to a staff of three. We recruited and hired a team of consultants to work with us over the long term to assist our portfolio nonprofits. Keystone Community Ventures provided our investees with business planning and financial analysis. CompuMentor, Dayspring Technologies, and Third Strand addressed technology infrastructure and database issues. We hired BTW Consultants to help us plan and implement our social outcome measurement efforts. We invited each of these consultants to be part of the monthly Information Management Team (IMT) meetings to make sure our capacity-building efforts were coordinated and consistent.

Each of these redesign efforts was underpinned by our fundamental strategy of providing large sums of annual, renewable, unrestricted funding to our investees ($150,000–$350,000 each year) and making long-term commitments (five-plus years). Most important, we ensured that all our capacity-building efforts resulted in knowledge transfer to the nonprofits. This may seem like a basic point about capacity building, but it can often look a lot easier to do something for a nonprofit partner than to truly build the knowledge base of a nonprofit to do it on its own. While REDF's particular approach to funding may not be as easily replicated, this emphasis on knowledge transfer is one that funders can all embrace—and screen consultants and staff for their ability to do so.

Charting the Path to an Information Oasis

Nonprofits are by nature social change experts, not social scientists. This presents a problem when we ask nonprofits to design systems to measure the results of their social change activities. We as funders can facilitate nonprofit skill development through the tar-geted use of consultants or deploying our own skilled staff to assess current capacity and encourage nonprofit staff to think about what change they expect to see as a result of their work. Starting with some basic questions about expected outcomes can lead over time to a mindset of using information to inform practice.

Our first step toward building our portfolio members' capacity for measurement was an assessment of each organization's capac-ity in the areas of business planning, financial analysis, technology, and social outcome measurement. Each consultant conducted an independent assessment and brought that information back to the IMT for discussion and decisions about next steps.

On the business planning and financial analysis fronts, our busi-ness consultant worked with each enterprise to develop a business plan and improve its financial reporting. REDF staff and the busi-ness consultant held monthly venture committee meetings with each portfolio organization. In these venture committee meetings, the executive director, controller, business managers, and an occa-sional board member met with REDF staff to review the budgeted-versus-actual enterprise financials. We also discussed the top issues facing the business and how REDF could assist in moving the busi-ness toward sustainability.

We decided to start measuring business results first and gradually ease the groups into collecting data on their enterprise employees. Even though we had stopped using the language of "evaluation," the groups were wary of REDF's expectations for social outcome mea-surement. We recognized that gaining buy-in to measure social out-comes would need to be a long-term, collaborative process.

Trekking Through WebTrack

The IMT set out to build a Web-based system that everyone (IMT, REDF staff and donors, portfolio nonprofit management teams) could use to track business, financial, and eventually social outcome infor-mation. Our hope was to build each organization's capacity over time to report on and analyze its own financial and social outcome data.

Knowing that the enterprise managers were highly motivated to expand their businesses, we started by asking them what kinds of data, in addition to standard financial indicators, would help them manage their enterprises. Our consulting team helped each business define appropriate operational indicators and figure out how to best collect this information.

Business Operations Indicators for the REDF Portfolio

Standard Financial Indicators

- Gross sales monthly
- Gross sales year-to-date
- Gross profit monthly
- Gross profit year-to-date
- Net profit before social costs and subsidy monthly
- Net profit before social costs and subsidy year-to-date
- Net profit including social costs and subsidy monthly
- Net profit including social costs and subsidy year-to-date

Customized Operations Indicators (Note: These are samples of monthly indicators that differed by enterprise.)

- Customer satisfaction
- Cost of goods sold
- Cost of direct labor
- Number of sales calls monthly
- Timely completion of jobs
- Revenue per square foot
- Inventory reliability
- Inventory turnover rate
- Production wastage

The WebTrack business indicator system took six months to develop and implement. Six months after the launch of WebTrack, the consulting team met with each of the enterprises to assess their usage of WebTrack and ask for recommendations. At this point, most of the enterprise staff responded positively to the WebTrack initiative.

WebTrack Woes. Fairly soon after we heard the initial positive response to WebTrack, however, things began to fall apart. Many portfolio enterprises stopped entering their data on a monthly basis or submitted the data late. Most of the input was inconsistent with other financial information we received in venture committee meetings. In addition, we at REDF could not keep up with the few data that were being reported, and no one was using the data to inform their practice.

To make matters worse, REDF staff found themselves in the role of hounding enterprise managers about the timeliness and accuracy of data. Literally—one staff member was officially designated as the "hounder" and had a cartoon of a hound dog on her bulletin board. REDF rapidly slid down the slippery slope of turning information management into a punitive system. At one point, REDF staff even threatened groups with the prospect of losing future grants if they did not enter their WebTrack data on time.

Within another six months, we realized how badly WebTrack had gone awry and called a time-out with the portfolio members. The IMT conducted another series of conversations with portfolio members to assess what, if any, components of WebTrack were worth saving and eventually ended up abandoning WebTrack altogether. One portfolio director commented that in retrospect, "WebTrack was REDF's transitional object."

Accounting for Change. It should come as no surprise that change takes time. Facilitating change in social outcome measurement systems, financial accounting systems, and organizational culture takes a lot of time and willingness from both nonprofits and funders to try new approaches and learn from failure together.

During the decline of WebTrack, we turned our attention to the accounting and financial management issues with our portfolio members. The WebTrack debacle made it clear that some enterprise managers did not understand how to read basic financial statements nor the importance of using the data to manage the business. One manager consistently entered in "0" for his monthly net income—thinking that was what REDF wanted to see, not realizing it was impossible that his enterprise would be exactly at breakeven month after month. Another executive director didn't see why being able to calculate the cost-of-goods-sold figure for his manufacturing business was essential. He therefore could not appreciate how problematic it was that his agency controller and accounting software could not generate this very important set of numbers.

The business consultant spent hours each week with enterprise managers and nonprofit controllers teaching them about income statement line items, formats, and the value of cash flow projections. Financial reporting continued to improve but also became more complex as the enterprises grew. Month after month, the venture committee meetings were dominated by heated debates about financial statement accuracy and the resulting implications for the management of the enterprise.

Beyond WebTrack: Financial Measurement

Although we had left WebTrack behind in the desert dust, we continued to forge ahead with our plans and refocused our attention on new ways to approach financial and social outcome measurement. Over time, REDF hired an accounting firm to work with the portfolio enterprises on assessing their financial systems and controls, make recommendations for software upgrades, and implement staff training. With the overall improvements in financial accounting and reports, REDF created an internal system called QTrack to track key financial data directly from the enterprise financial statements received in the venture committee meetings. We also developed a regular schedule for analyzing and reporting out on the data both to REDF staff and to the portfolio organizations.

Beyond WebTrack: Social Outcome Measurement

In 1998, BTW Consultants began collecting basic aggregate employee information across each enterprise. This census type data included items such as age, gender, ethnicity, and the number of employees who joined or left an enterprise in a given quarter.

We also began an extensive social impact study of portfolio enterprise employees. We asked each organization and enterprise what social outcomes they expected to see in the lives of their employees over time. We mapped this information across the portfolio, identified the crosscutting outcome areas, and listed other areas that REDF in particular wanted to track.

We then created a core set of questions that would be asked of each portfolio enterprise employee at the time of hire and at six-month increments up to two years post-hire—regardless of whether the employee still worked at that portfolio enterprise.

Core Social Impact Indicators

- Job retention
- Job placement
- Job promotion
- Wages
- Barriers to employment
- Reliance on public assistance
- Use of social services
- Housing stability
- Self-esteem
- Personal support
- Involvement in the criminal justice system
- A full complement of demographic characteristics

In exchange for participating in this social outcome measurement effort, we offered each organization the opportunity to add additional outcome areas it was interested in tracking and offered to fund the entire cost of the core and customized social outcome measurement process.

Most portfolio organizations were responsive to the offer of social impact measurement and customization. In fact, originally REDF suggested only half the portfolio enterprises be included in the social impact assessment, and in response, the organizations requested that all of their enterprises be included. In the end, every new employee in fifteen REDF portfolio enterprises was tracked from 1998 forward.

Collecting Dew from Cactus: The Aggregate Data Collection Process

The aggregate data collection system only took two months to develop and implement. We thought it would be an easy way for the groups to gather timely, accurate data on their enterprise employees. What soon became clear was that obtaining these data was like collecting dew from cactus—it was a slow and painful process.

Portfolio enterprises experienced high employee turnover, and employees were spread across several different enterprise locations. It was difficult for the organizations to count how many employees they had on a given day, not to mention a quarter's worth of demographic data on the overall employee population. One organization had to go through all its personnel files and manually count how many employees each of its enterprises had employed and hand tally the demographics. Another had to go through each employee's pay stubs to report on the wage range paid each quarter. One of our nonprofit executive directors exclaimed one day in frustration, "I wish I could just press a button and get all this information!" REDF had no immediate solution for this, but we kept the comment in mind for the future.

The Land Rover: The Individual Social Impact Data Collection System

The social impact data collection system took from 1997 to 1998 to develop and implement. While this system was far more complicated than the aggregate data collection system, overall it was perhaps easier for groups to adopt. Key to this adoption were well-planned buy-in strategies and incentives and more accurate collective expectations about the time and resources required for its implementation.

We made grants to each organization to cover staff time required for planning and implementation. We budgeted significant resources to allow the social outcome consultants to teach and train the groups on outcome measurement. We bought gift certificates to reward enterprise employees for participating in the outcome survey. We created customized automated databases for each group so they could submit and receive all the data they needed from the social outcome consultants over the Internet. We bent over backward to ensure we had a collaborative process and tried to be as flexible as possible in accommodating special requests. We built a Land Rover version of an enterprise social outcome measurement system when perhaps a Jeep would have sufficed.

The Land Rover Limitation

When the IMT offered to customize the social impact data collection system, we received some interesting requests. One organization wanted to ask three hundred questions instead of the forty core questions and wanted to track all three thousand clients instead of just the hundred enterprise employees. Another organization wanted to streamline the way it reported on social outcomes to all funders, not just REDF. Yet another organization wanted to assess whether the services it provided to enterprise employees were having an impact. Additionally, the organization wanted to tie those outcomes to the financial investment required to support both the enterprise and the services to calculate the SROI. In contrast, two other organizations made it clear they did not want to customize their data at all, and they were only participating in the social outcome data collection process out of obligation.

The Land Rover social impact data collection system only focused on enterprise employment outcomes and could not help the entire organization build its capacity for measurement. Although the nonprofits already knew this, it was a revelation to REDF. Armed with this information, we began the final search for an information oasis along with our portfolio organizations.

At Last, an Information OASIS

In 1999, we began the OASIS (Ongoing Assessment of Social ImpactS) project. OASIS, by definition, was about building a customized, comprehensive social management information system (social MIS) within each nonprofit organization. OASIS was designed to be both a process and a product. It captures every client served by the entire agency, not just enterprise employees, and involves a reengineering of how each agency delivers its services. The project spanned the areas of overall nonprofit service delivery, client tracking and outcomes, staff interventions and performance, program delivery and performance, and all reporting requirements to all funders.

The OASIS project involved the same IMT and REDF portfolio organizations in a multiyear, multimillion-dollar organizational capacity-building process. REDF raised $2 million from other foundations to fund the majority of the costs of each phase of OASIS with each portfolio member. The OASIS project went through nine phases:

1. Assessing organizational readiness to pursue OASIS

2. Convening a working group with the organization

3. Identifying key staff within each nonprofit organization

4. Establishing consulting partnerships

5. Assessing organizational client-related information needs

6. Designing the client-tracking system

7. Equipping the organization with appropriate technology infrastructure

8. Automating the client-tracking system

9. Implementing OASIS and operating the system

Many of the lessons we had learned from our past measurement efforts were incorporated into the OASIS implementation. We started with six organizations participating in OASIS, and as of 2002, four of them were still at various stages of planning and implementation. We've learned a great deal in the course of all this, but overall OASIS has been a success and a culmination of our best practices around social outcome measurement.

The Information Oasis: A Life-Changing Destination for Nonprofits

Many changes have occurred in the lives of the nonprofit organizations that have created cultures of measurement. It has influenced how their organizations do their work on a day-to-day basis in both dramatic and subtle ways.

The benefits of having timely and accurate financial statements across an organization are more obvious—having better financial data enables managers to see clearly which programs and enterprises are sustainable and which ones are losing money—and make decisions accordingly. The organization can be more forward-thinking and strategic about its fundraising efforts and expansion plans with accurate financial information.

The benefits of having timely and accurate social outcome reports across an organization have been more surprising and dramatic in many ways. One REDF portfolio director recently talked about how OASIS has transformed her organization in three major ways:

> It has streamlined all of our paperwork and processes. We went from using 140 different forms to track our clients down to 36 forms—a more than 300 percent reduction in paperwork.
>
> It has increased our response to problem areas. It has turned our agency into a more dynamic organization by providing easily accessible and up-to-date outcome reports on every program we run. This allows us to identify and respond to challenging areas before they become a problem.
>
> It has made it easier for our staff to do their jobs. We can track which programs our clients are in, what progress they've made, which staff are working with which clients, and we can pull data from the system in a quick and organized manner to compile customized reports for each funding source.

Other portfolio directors have commented how having timely and accurate measurement systems has made them more competitive in fundraising proposals. Their systems provide data and reports that have far more statistical validity than what funders expect to receive from nonprofits. In addition, their systems have served in part to level the playing field between the organizations and potential funders. The nonprofits are clearer about what kinds of outcomes they can generate from their programs and therefore are clear about which grants they can pursue or accept from funders.

The ongoing analyses and reflection on the data are helping to improve service delivery to their clients and informing their program development to better meet their mission. The search for an information oasis has resulted in many tangible benefits for REDF and for the nonprofits we fund—and it is helping us to more effectively serve the most vulnerable members of our society.

Seven Lessons from the Search: A Jeep Conclusion

As noted earlier, at the end of the day we as funders must be able to answer the question, How do you know your work makes a difference? We cannot afford to not measure our own results and those of the nonprofits we fund, and yet we must be mindful of using our precious resources in the wisest way possible in measuring impact. In sharing our lessons we hope to help other funders avoid the mistakes we made during our long search for an information oasis and contribute to ongoing efforts to build a more effective nonprofit sector.

Lesson 1: A foundation can best cultivate a culture of measurement within the nonprofits it funds by cultivating a culture of measurement within itself.

We as funders cannot expect the nonprofits we fund to create a culture of measurement if we do not have such a culture within our own institutions. How can we expect more of our grantees, in the area of measurement or any other area for that matter, than we expect of our own organizations? Regardless of our foundations' size or scope, we need to follow our own recommendations before we ask our grantees to join us in the effort.

REDF has always been numbers-driven. Part of this has to do with the nature of our investment in nonprofit-run enterprises. We also have a donor who consistently asks complex questions about calculating the impact of REDF's work.

Our donor's questions have spanned impact areas including outputs, financial performance, quantitative and qualitative social outcomes, organizational capacity built, SROI, cost-effectiveness, and competitive benchmarking in each of these areas. We are constantly searching for more data on the enterprises, from the field, and on the value of our funding strategy to our investees in order to inform our practice of philanthropy.

REDF Measures of Performance

REDF has measured the impact of its investments in social purpose enterprise organizations and its own impact in multiple ways to date:

- Collecting quarterly aggregate information on the mission-related employees of each portfolio enterprise

- Collecting and analyzing social outcome information on new hires

- Collecting and analyzing monthly income statement information

- Combining the first three measures into a social return on investment (SROI) model

- Assessing REDF's impact on overall organizational effectiveness within portfolio members

- Examining the cost-effectiveness of REDF's approach versus other similar approaches

- Studying the relationship between specific employee social outcomes and the types of social purpose enterprises that employ these individuals

Over the years, as we at REDF have pursued our own information oasis, many of the groups we fund have joined us in this search. In a retrospective assessment of REDF's impact on its portfolio organizations from 1997 to 2001, four executive directors credited REDF as a significant catalyst for creating a culture of measurement within their organizations.

One director commented, "[REDF brought a] culture, a language of discipline. . . . The venture committee meetings . . . spilled over to the social program staff area." In this particular agency, based on the social outcome and financial cost data collected, the management decided to close a beloved program that had proved to be ineffective and costly. While this decision was not popular with some members of the nonprofit's board, the data made it very clear that resources within the agency could be more effectively deployed to serve clients in other ways.

Another REDF-funded organization director said, "As a result, our board, our staff, and even the people we serve have changed in the way they use information." Yet another director added, "REDF's expectations and business mentality raised performance across the agency. . . . Last year we implemented goals across the agency. We're more numbers-driven now while maintaining our passion for people. . . . There's more accountability across the agency . . . now everyone has REDF expectations."

Questions for Funders

- Do we have a culture of measurement?
- Is there broad accountability for financial and social outcome reporting?
- Does this information inform grantmaking practice?
- How does our board assess our own successes or failures in grantmaking?
- Is there a commitment to self-examination among the staff and board?

Lesson 2: Cultivating a culture of measurement takes time—longer than you might think!

As with most activities worth pursuing in life, creating timely and accurate financial and social outcome measurement systems took a lot longer than any of us expected. Change, and especially culture change within organizations, takes time.

For each stage of the process, whether building WebTrack, getting financial systems in order, helping our nonprofits adopt the social impact data collection system, or implementing OASIS, the time required to completion was consistently extended. For example, we declared 1998 our "year of accounting"—thinking that surely by the end of the year we would have timely and accurate financial statements from each of our portfolio organizations. Now—five years later—we are finally seeing the fruit from all our labor.

We learned several key lessons along the way:

- Start out gradually.
- Set expectations early.
- Conduct regular check-ins and gather feedback.
- Establish long-term partnerships.

Start Out Gradually. We can only imagine what a disaster we would have created if we had tried to pursue all our data collection and measurement efforts at once. Other foundations have looked at our list of measurement activities and wonder how we do it all. The answer is that we did not do it all at once. We started out with collecting basic census data on our enterprises and then moved on to collect enterprise social outcome data and then organization-wide outcome data. On the financial side, we started with basic financial statements in the beginning; then, over time, we helped build the nonprofit's capacity for more sophisticated financial reporting and complex accounting systems. By gradually increasing the complexity of our work on measurement with the groups, we were able to demonstrate the value of smaller sets of information and prepare the groups for the next step.

Set Expectations Early. We made many mistakes when we started setting expectations and learned from these mistakes the hard way. WebTrack was a disaster because we did not talk with our portfolio members about whether they even wanted or knew how to use a Web-based system to enter data. The aggregate data collection process was slow and painful for the groups. It did not work because we had not discussed with them how they would collect these data, we just assumed it would be simple for them to do.

In contrast, the social outcome data collection went relatively smoothly with the participating groups. The difference was largely due to our up-front efforts in planning with the nonprofits about what the process would be and how much time it would take them to implement the social outcome data collection system. We had numerous meetings and conversations with the nonprofit staff to understand how their current systems worked (or didn't work) and how we could help them build a process and a system that would not create too much burden on staff. Additionally, based on our mutual assessment of the time required for staff to participate in the planning meetings and implementation process, we funded their staff costs accordingly.

Conduct Regular Check-Ins and Gather Feedback. This recommendation may seem rather obvious, but after multiple missteps and miscommunications between our staff, our consultants, and nonprofit management and staff in the past, we cannot overemphasize the importance of regular communication and asking portfolio members how the process is going. Our regular check-ins have brought about changes to our measurement activities mid-course and significantly altered the way in which we work with our portfolio members. As a result, we have articulated five C's as guiding principles for how we do our work with our portfolio members: Clarity in Communication, Customization, and Collaboration in our approach, and Consistency in everything we do.

Over the years, we have conducted regular check-ins with our portfolio members. It may seem excessive, but given the number of activities we are engaged in with our portfolio members we have all agreed that it is not possible to communicate too much with each other. The IMT members each check in with the groups regularly, and REDF's business assistance staff meets with portfolio business managers on a monthly basis. REDF's managing director meets quarterly with each portfolio agency director, and all this is on top of the monthly venture committee meetings and frequent e-mail correspondence. We have found these constant interactions are essential to our ultimate success in that they enable us to gather feedback on changing progress and expectations in real time.

Establish Long-Term Partnerships. We believe lasting changes to organizational culture are best cultivated in the context of long-term partnerships. Effecting lasting change takes time, resources, and significant coordination on the part of both the funder and the nonprofit organization. The REDF portfolio organizations that have successfully cultivated a culture of measurement have been partners with REDF for six to twelve years. The process has been a participatory one, with great flexibility on each party's side to respond to the other's feedback and to be willing to change.

REDF and our portfolio management teams have been holding monthly venture committee meetings since 1997. This has meant gathering together all the key decision makers regarding the social purpose enterprises in the same room at the same time, every month, year after year. Through these venture committee meetings, we have collectively instilled the discipline of gathering financial data, reflecting on the data, and making decisions together based on the data. The discipline of the monthly venture committee meetings over the years has served to elevate the role of data use and reflection to inform nonprofit practice and ultimately in promoting a culture of measurement.

Recently, a local foundation was impressed with the kinds of social outcome data that one of the REDF portfolio members was able to produce in comparison to other nonprofits in its funded portfolio. Its staff gathered their grantees together and showcased this one nonprofit's outcome reports and requested that the other grantees produce the same kinds of data before the funded project ended in three months. This foundation had many resources to devote to this effort but lacked the time or the context of a long-term partnership within which to develop a culture change in the nonprofits. The REDF portfolio member's director later commented, "[The other foundation] had a lot of resources, but we had to emphasize to them that [social outcome measurement] is a process as well as a product. It takes time to get it right. It takes institutional commitment, which in a funny way is the most valuable resource. You can't buy institutional commitment."

The value of time cannot be understated. As this same nonprofit director commented, "[Ultimately, our organization] embraced a culture of measurement. Information is valued across the organization; it improves people's work. [REDF] gave us the luxury of time to get it right." While not all funders can provide their grantees with longer-term funding and the luxury of time to get things right, there are other ways to help cultivate a culture of measurement in the short run. Simply asking good questions about what outcomes a nonprofit expects to see as a result of its work instead of stating what outcomes your foundation would like to see it achieve can help change the mindset of the nonprofit. In all of this, it is important to be clear about what is reasonable to expect in what time frame. Change does take time. But change also happens one step at a time, and different funders in communication with each other can help effect lasting change through a series of coordinated short-term efforts.

Questions for Funders

- How do we set expectations with our grantees about our financial and social outcome reporting requirements?

- Have we ever asked our grantees how long it takes them and what steps they need to go through to provide the reports we require?

- Have we ever asked our grantees how we could help them provide us with timely, accurate reports?

- How often do we ask grantees for feedback on our grantmaking practices overall?

- What kinds of things can we do in the short term to help promote long-term culture change around measurement?

- Are we willing and able to make longer-term commitments to our grantees to give them the luxury of time to "get it right"?

Lesson 3: Cultivating a culture of measurement takes significant resources, appropriate incentives, and lots of coordination.

Significant Resources. Each year at REDF we devote substantial resources toward our financial and social outcome measurement efforts. REDF hires individuals (primarily MBAs) with strong business backgrounds to work directly with our portfolio members. Three REDF staff members meet monthly with each nonprofit management team to review financial information and help them build their enterprises. REDF has hired an accounting firm to work with all the portfolio organizations to ensure their financial systems are in order and assist them with ongoing projects to improve their accounting systems. REDF has also been involved in helping to identify, recruit, and retain key financial management staff, including CFOs and controllers, and funds a bonus program for enterprise managers and executive directors.

Ten percent of REDF's annual budget, or approximately $350,000 a year, is dedicated to funding REDF's capacity-building efforts around social outcome measurement alone. This amount covers the work the social outcome consultants do with REDF staff and portfolio members to collect, analyze, and teach people to use the data, and some of the social outcome measurement capacity-building grants made to portfolio members.

The social outcome consultants focus on three major activities related to building organizational capacity:

- Gathering data

  Training staff on survey methods and techniques

  Developing custom databases to house information at the nonprofit once collected

- Analyzing data

  Training staff in basic statistical analysis

  Developing a Web-accessed follow-up report form that will allow each organization access to its own outcome data and generate basic reports

- Using data

  Presenting data in easy-to-understand formats such as newsletters and PowerPoint presentations

  Training on how to understand the data by conducting interactive sessions with staff

  Tying performance reviews and compensation to individual staff members' ability to gather, analyze, and use data to improve nonprofit practice

Appropriate Incentives. Another resource-intensive but key component has been developing appropriate incentives for mea-surement at all levels. To cultivate a culture of measurement within our portfolio organizations as well as within REDF itself, we built in incentive systems throughout our measurement activities. These incentives range from gift certificates given to enterprise target employees who respond to our social outcome measurement surveys to rewards for REDF staff for their diligence in pursuing all kinds of measurement activities. Each of these incentive systems has generated positive results.

Lots of Coordination. Lastly, resources invested in capacity building should be well coordinated across multiple fronts. At REDF, the composition of the IMT and the monthly IMT meetings have played essential roles in keeping our strategy and communications consistent over time. We have seen the synergies of simultaneously building capacity in technology, social outcome measurement, and financial management.

From 1997 to 2001, the IMT met monthly to review progress, troubleshoot issues, discuss changes to social outcome data collection efforts, and report on feedback from individual groups. REDF's director led the meetings, set the agendas, and ensured that all the consultants were on track. In addition to the regular IMT meetings, REDF's director met with each consultant one-on-one at least every six months to ensure individual efforts were of the highest quality and to follow up with any issues raised by the portfolio members regarding the consultant. The IMT also maintained an e-mail discussion list to facilitate shared communication among the different consulting groups and REDF staff. The consultants developed their annual budgets together to ensure adequate resources were available for each portfolio member.

Building capacity on the financial measurement side required similar levels of coordination. For example, we encouraged one organization to improve its financial reporting capacity by simultaneously purchasing a new financial software package, paying for consultants and training for accounting staff, funding salaries for accounting staff, and including the nonprofit's chief financial officer in an incentive program to encourage specific changes in the accounting system.

All these coordinated efforts are necessary to assist an organization in building its capacity for financial and social outcome measurement and, again, ensuring the incentives are in place to cultivate a culture of measurement.

These multiple examples may seem rather overwhelming in their scope and resource requirements—and especially in the context of a single funder's efforts to build an organization's capacity for measurement. Some funders may consider piloting a smaller-scale capacity-building initiative within a single program area, instead of an entire organization, in an effort to bring about some culture change within a smaller area of the nonprofit. Other funders may want to experiment with choosing a particular area such as outcome measurement within a specific program area and see what changes can be brought about.

Questions for Funders

- How much of our budget is allocated for capacity-building efforts?

- How much of our budget is allocated for financial and social outcome measurement activities?

- What percentage of a funded grant goes toward the nonprofit's measurement activities?

- What kinds of incentives do we fund for nonprofits to pursue measurement activities?

- What kinds of incentives do we have in place to encourage our staff to measure their own results in grantmaking?

Lesson 4: Organizations need to be ready for change.

Funders and nonprofit organizations both need to be ready to pursue a culture of measurement together. REDF had to model a culture of measurement if we were to influence the organizations in which we invested, and the organizations had to want it for themselves.

One nonprofit we funded over several years was not successful in cultivating a culture of measurement. We had the suspicion that if measured, the organization's impact would prove to be less significant than it had advertised to its many funders—and perhaps the executive director shared this suspicion. We invested large sums of money and hours of BTW Consultants' time to help this organization measure its social outcomes, with little follow-through or results.

This lack of interest in social outcome accountability also applied to the financial accounting side of the organization. We pressed the organization's director for timely, accurate financial information on the enterprises, requested that he build his accounting department capacity, and even offered to fund a chief financial officer position, all to no avail. In the end, it became clear that the organization had taken on more debt than it could support and was in a serious cash flow crisis—and had successfully masked this fact from its board of directors. Ultimately, to meet its debt obligations the organization had to implement massive layoffs and divest most of its hard assets, including its social purpose enterprises.

In this and several other examples, we have observed that any enthusiasm for or resistance to using data we find on the financial side of an organization is mirrored on the social outcome and program side of the organization, and vice versa. Organizations and their leadership must have some appetite for the truth and the accountability that comes with better information. Cultures of measurement (or not) are truly pervasive.

The following checklist can help assess whether an organization is ready:

Organizational Readiness Checklist

- The leadership—executive director and management—is committed to measurement planning and product.
- The organization is relatively stable with respect to leadership and programs.
- The organization is able to commit staff time to planning efforts.
- The organization has a culture that values information about financial stability, service delivery, and social impact.
- The organization has sufficient financial resources to devote to the effort, both for the development stage and for future sustainability.
- The organization has consulting partnerships in place to assist in the different phases of development.

If even one of these aspects is missing, it will be difficult, if not impossible, to successfully cultivate a culture of measurement.

Questions for Funders

- Looking at the organizational readiness checklist, are we missing any of these important aspects of readiness to embrace a culture of measurement?

- Assessing the nonprofits we fund against the organizational readiness checklist, how many of our grantees are ready to change their organizational cultures? What can we do to help nonprofits start down the path toward a culture of measurement?

Lesson 5: Technology is not the (entire) answer.

In this age of ever-improving technology, it is tempting to see technology as the solution to our efforts at measuring both financial and social outcomes. While equipping nonprofits with appropriate technology is important, technology alone is not the solution to cultivate a culture of measurement. Customized databases, off-the-shelf social outcome software packages, and sleek accounting systems are simply tools that must be accompanied by appropriate staffing, training, and careful attention to adoption rates and change management if they are to be truly useful. Some funders, REDF included, sometimes become enamored of the latest technology without recognizing the limitations of our nonprofit partners in properly employing that technology and the implications of adopting too much technology too quickly.

The creation of REDF's WebTrack system was primarily driven by REDF's desire to replicate a social outcomes technology we had seen in the Pacific Northwest. As a result, in 1997, the IMT developed WebTrack as a Web-based solution for tracking financial and social outcome information across the portfolio. Based on assessments we did at the time, it was clear that to make WebTrack operational, we needed to build the portfolio organizations' capacity to use technology effectively, as most of the nonprofits had limited access to PCs and few had e-mail or access to the Internet.

We equipped each enterprise with the basic hardware and software needed for their business operations and provided them with access to e-mail and the Internet. Our technology consultants installed the hardware and software and taught people how to use e-mail. We budgeted a small amount for each organization to access ongoing technical support. REDF staff started using e-mail as the primary vehicle for communication in order to encourage portfolio members to check their e-mail. As an incentive for checking e-mail frequently, we would send out regular "Easter eggs" through the portfolio's e-mail discussion group, offering baseball or symphony tickets to the first responders. It may seem funny today to have to provide incentives for people to check their e-mail, but back in 1997 it was absolutely necessary to encourage technology adoption.

The technology consultants built WebTrack as a private Web site with an information management system and successive layers of password protection that allowed each group to enter in its own business and financial data online and, with a push of a button, submit that information to the IMT. The IMT also had a password-protected area on WebTrack where IMT members and REDF's donor could view individual and aggregated business and financial data for every enterprise in the portfolio.

We expected that business managers would become used to the idea of tracking information on the Web on a monthly basis, reporting it, having it analyzed by the business consultant and REDF staff and then reflecting on it with REDF staff at the monthly venture committee meetings. By the end of 1997, however, it was clear that the portfolio organizations had not embraced the use of e-mail and the Internet in their daily lives. Creating a cutting-edge technology for reporting data did not result in better measurement practices.

We realized in retrospect that building WebTrack for our portfolio members was analogous to purchasing a piece of high-end financial accounting software for an agency without covering the basics:

- A system to receive, record, input, and quality check data
- Staff who understand and know how to input financial data accurately
- Staff who can analyze financial data to determine the financial health of programs and organization
- Incentives in place for staff to value accurate, timely financial information
- Leadership that demonstrates it values accurate, timely financial information by asking for it and using it to make decisions
- An organizational commitment to use the data to inform practice

Our lessons learned about the limitations of technology in creating culture change spanned both the social outcome and the financial reporting realms.

Questions for Funders

- Is there a mismatch between the level of technology used in our foundation and that in our grantees?

- Are we currently making technology grants that are not tied to other activities that would support the effective use of that technology within the nonprofit organization?

Lesson 6: Beware the slippery slope of evaluation—resist turning evaluation into a punitive system.

Evaluation in its funder-imposed, retrospective, punitive form is pervasive in the nonprofit sector. As the saying goes, "Old habits die hard"—and evaluation is definitely one of the old habits of the grantmaking world. Using a new language of *outcome measurement* or *social MIS* can be helpful—but only to the extent that actions are consistent with those words. REDF was adamant about never using the word *evaluation* in our work. ("Evaluation is a bad word" even became a running joke between REDF and our portfolio members.) Yet before we realized what was happening, we'd turned WebTrack into a punitive system. It is essential for funders to be constantly self-critical and ask for regular feedback from nonprofit partners to ensure that measurement efforts are informing nonprofit practice. It is equally essential that funders be willing to hear negative feedback and be quick to change—modeling a culture of using data to inform practice.

An interesting problem has developed for REDF portfolio organizations that now have more accurate social outcome information on their programs. The slightly unintended effect of having great social outcome measurement systems is that the numbers they are reporting are not quite as positive as what funders are used to seeing. Other grantmaking staff ask, "Why are you only placing 64 percent of the people you train when you said you would place 80 percent?" To which the nonprofit staff respond, "We're being honest with you about our actual outcomes. Our grant proposal projected our best guess as to what they would be, and we are working to increase our placement rate."

Foundations have become so accustomed to seeing nonprofits report successful outcomes most of the time that it is a shock to see a nonprofit report less than stellar numbers. We as funders need to be careful not to punish organizations that are finally doing what we've wanted them to do for so long—produce accurate social outcome reports—just because we don't like the numbers we see. Embracing a culture of measurement for the nonprofit sector will need to involve a significant change in the way funders analyze data, reflect on data, and react to the data for future funding decisions.

Questions for Funders

- How do we approach our evaluation efforts?

- Is evaluation imposed on the nonprofits we fund, or do we engage them in a discussion of what the appropriate outcomes should be and develop an evaluation strategy together?

Lesson 7: Information only makes a difference if it is used.

How many of us well-meaning funders have asked for, and received from our grantees, data that we then never reviewed? How much capacity do we as funders have for data? And how much data can we expect nonprofits to produce and review and digest in order to assess how well their programs are delivering results? The truth is that many funders have reams and reams of reports from their grantees that live in filing cabinets and are not informing nonprofit or funder practice.

From the beginning, REDF wanted the information we gathered from our funded organizations to inform our collective practice. We did not want the information to end up in written reports on dusty bookshelves in our respective offices. Despite these desires, we fell into a couple of data traps along the way.

Everyone Wants More Data Than They Can Use. Nonprofits, given the opportunity, will want to collect more data than they can possibly take in. We found this to be true with the development of the WebTrack business indicators, the customization of the enterprise survey, and the overall scope of the OASIS project. In each case, given the opportunity presented by REDF, the nonprofits wanted to collect far more information than they could reasonably consume, and therefore the data were not ultimately useful. We needed to help the nonprofits be more realistic about what data they could really use to inform practice.

Too Much Data Will Land with a Thud. In 2000, when BTW Consultants generated our first portfolio-wide social outcome report, they included data gathered since 1998 on all the employees of the fifteen portfolio enterprises across seven outcome areas. There was a substantial "thud" factor to the report—it offered so much data and analysis, we could not take it all in. This report is sitting in a binder somewhere on a dusty bookshelf in our office.

Based on this experience, we and BTW Consultants have learned over time how to use all this information more effectively. REDF now has each organization and enterprise's social outcome data summarized in PowerPoint presentations and reader-friendly newsletters. BTW presents and discusses this information with each portfolio organization on a quarterly basis. REDF staff meet quarterly with BTW to discuss the data on a single outcome area and reflect on its implications for our work. REDF's managing director meets quarterly with the principal of BTW to talk about the big picture issues related to the social outcome data.

Since the demise of WebTrack, all the financial data by enterprise by month have been entered into QTrack, a database located at REDF. A staff member systematically analyzes these data for business trends and issues over time. REDF business assistance staff meet weekly to discuss the financial data and other information coming from their interactions with portfolio members at venture committee meetings and other sessions. All these data and conversations inform REDF's practice with its portfolio enterprises.

Additionally, REDF staff and all nonprofit management staff meet together quarterly to discuss the portfolio-wide data and their implications for the field of social purpose enterprise. Finally, every six months, REDF staff present the financial and social outcome results on each enterprise to George R. Roberts, REDF's founder and donor. These six-month reports and the discussions that follow direct REDF's future strategies and funding. There is little doubt that the data are being used.

Questions for Funders

- Do we ask for more data from our grantees than we can consume?
- Have we built time for reflection into our work to ensure we are using the data we do have to inform our practice?
- How can we build in time for collective reflection with our grantees about their outcomes?

Conclusion: The Continuing Quest for a Sector-Wide Information Oasis

We need to cultivate a culture of measurement across the entire nonprofit sector, including both philanthropic and nonprofit organizations, even if it means doing so organization by organization. If we as funders expect the nonprofits we fund to embrace greater accountability and demonstrate their financial and social outcomes in a timely and accurate way, we ourselves must be ready to change.

The philanthropic community has become used to a culture of personality, politics, and persuasion that drives funding decisions in the nonprofit sector. Having nonprofits that produce real information on actual outcomes may come as a shock to us when it does happen. Nonprofits must want to know if they are really making a difference in measurable, quantifiable ways. Grantmakers must want to know the truth about whether their grant dollars really made an impact. Grantmaking staff must to be willing to report less-than-stellar successes and, yes, even some spectacular failures in funding to their board members and trustees. Grantmaking boards and trustees need to be more risk-tolerant and information-driven in their grantmaking strategies. They must be willing to hear that a pet project isn't really achieving the social impact the foundation desires—and redirect funding elsewhere.

Accurate and timely information about nonprofit organizations' financial health and the impact of their programs and services is essential to building an effective nonprofit sector. Funders have a real opportunity to partner with the nonprofit organizations we fund to cultivate cultures of measurement. We at REDF are constantly collecting new data, learning new lessons, having those data inform our practice, and sharing our lessons learned with the field. We invite you to visit our Web site at www.redf.org to see how we're planning for our next trek and join us in a sector-wide search for an information oasis.

Afterword

Funding Effectiveness
for the Long Haul

Rick Cohen, Executive Director,
National Committee for Responsive Philanthropy

Fortunately for all of us toiling away among nonprofits, funders are a lot smarter than they used to be about what it takes to make nonprofit organizations more effective. Due to the leadership of people like Barbara Kibbe during her tenure with the David and Lucile Packard Foundation, discussion of "organizational effectiveness" has filtered into the content of nearly every recent major funder gathering and has been elevated to a position of credibility and importance with the growth and advancement of Grantmakers for Effective Organizations.

Nonetheless, the funder experience contained in this book actually represents a small portion of institutional funders, the remainder watching and perhaps learning but not necessarily incorporating, internalizing, and delivering in the most effective ways. To be sure, funding organizational effectiveness is precarious, shown to be easily excised from the grant portfolios of even the most major funders of organizational effectiveness when financial constraints force them to choose between funding effectiveness or supporting programs. It may be accurate to suggest that funder support for organizational effectiveness grantmaking is a mile wide and still only an inch deep—or maybe now a couple of inches due to GEO's work.

Among grassroots nonprofits, there is still disquiet about the effectiveness of the kinds of funder practices described by the authors. The sector has a long way to go, not just in bolstering the efforts outlined in this volume but in filling the gaps these practices have yet to fully address. A few of the gaps are worth discussion, and funders and nonprofits alike can do much to help fill them in.

Evaluating the effectiveness of the capacity builders. A recent national survey of nonprofit executives revealed they were overwhelmingly far less positive about the results of technical assistance interventions than were the assistance providers themselves—and their funders. That negative feedback is remarkably important to hear and absorb. The feedback loop on effectiveness interventions by the experts, despite the good efforts of some funders described in this volume, is flimsy or sometimes virtually nonexistent.

Credibility through research and analysis. A session at a recent conference of nonprofit technical assistance providers examined and revealed how few could articulate their framework for understanding, diagnosing, and intervening in nonprofit organizations to build effectiveness. While some top-notch interveners, routinely employed by funders and nonprofits on these issues, showed they knew what they were talking about, the vague understanding and jargon of many others revealed the wide variations in quality and depth in the field. The stronger management support organizations, technical assistance providers, and funders engaged in nonprofit effectiveness appeared to be those that were constantly examining and reexamining the structure, dynamics, and issues facing nonprofits and conducting hard research on critical issues in the field.

Effectiveness for nonprofit public policy advocacy and organizing. The National Committee for Responsive Philanthropy has surveyed nonprofits engaged in community organizing, political activism, "movement building," and social change advocacy for their attitudes toward funders' and technical assistance providers' understanding of the constraints nonprofits face in improving or maintaining their effectiveness. The overwhelming response was a sense that funders by and large do not "get" the capacity and effectiveness needs of organizing and advocacy groups. Instead they prescribe and fund capacity building suited to service deliverers rather than advocates.

Frances Kunreuther and her colleagues at the Hauser Center for Nonprofits at Harvard University have devoted extensive efforts toward better understanding the capacity needs of "movement" organizations, noting organizational effectiveness needs such as these:

- Developing a theory or model of social change that can be used to assess these organizations' effectiveness as nonprofit change agents
- Paying attention to mobilizing and involving constituents in ways more fundamental than the all-too-common "consumer satisfaction" focus
- Addressing the different kinds and trajectories of burnout and the challenges of involving people from different generations in social movement organizations
- Understanding and implementing accountability in this kind of work

Based on Kunreuther's movement-building research and NCRP's nonprofit advocacy surveys, it appears that the social change piece of the nonprofit sector has yet to find in the organizational effectiveness movement much relevance to its specific needs and challenges.

Gender, sexual orientation, race, ethnicity, class—diversity in the field. The respondents to NCRP's surveys in New York City, largely grassroots organizations working with racial and ethnic minority populations and immigrant groups, bemoaned the lack of racial or ethnic symmetry between them and the nonprofit effectiveness industry, including the grantmakers who support this work. Only 2.2 percent of family foundation board members are minorities; only 5.4 percent of all foundation CEOs are minorities—in a nation that will be 50 percent minority by 2050 or earlier. Less than 13 percent of the paid staff of private noncorporate foundations are African American, approximately 5.5 percent are Hispanic, and only 3.2 percent Asian or Pacific Islander, with a propensity particularly among African Americans for nearly two-fifths of foundation jobs to be "assistants" or "administrative support." Given the philanthropic sector's still inadequate performance regarding its own racial and ethnic diversity, funders should redouble their efforts to bring diversity to the avenues they create for building nonprofit effectiveness.

Broadening the base of support for effectiveness through inclusion of government. As with many funder-generated treatises, the authors of this volume call for attention to diversifying nonprofit revenues, which presumably would include leveraging government dollars, but pay scant attention to bringing governmental agencies to the table as partners committed to building long-term, sustainable nonprofit organizations. Sometimes funders get so absorbed in their own spheres of activity, they fail to notice comparable efforts in the public sector that would be hugely enhanced if foundations viewed government as an important, logical, and necessary partner—especially since public sector revenues dwarf foundation grants in nonprofit budgets across the sector.

Under both Republican and Democratic administrations since the Carter era, the federal government has committed millions of dollars to capacity building for nonprofit community development corporations, community development financial institutions, community housing development organizations, and other categories of nonprofits. Some funders have seen the light and brought government into the organizational effectiveness process. For example, the U.S. Department of Housing and Urban Development is a full partner of Living Cities (more widely known as the National Community Development Initiative), a project of several funders including the John S. and James L. Knight Foundation, the Rockefeller Foundation, the McKnight Foundation, the John D. and Catherine T. MacArthur Foundation, the Annie E. Casey Foundation, the Surdna Foundation, Bank of America, and the Fannie Mae Foundation.

At the local and metropolitan level, the Ford Foundation has long pioneered the concept of multi-funder operating support collaboratives or partnerships, providing a combination of technical assistance and operating support for nonprofit community development corporations. Operating in some three dozen cities, these collaboratives increasingly involve local government agencies committing HOME, Community Development Block Grant, and other dollars to the efforts. The participating foundations and government agencies have learned from one another. The foundations take on higher-risk ventures or address thorny issues if they are sharing the investment and capacity-building risk, and the governments depoliticize their operating support and capacity-building money if they are in partnership with thoughtful philanthropic partners. Funders committed to nonprofit organizational effectiveness have to be attentive to the roles of all funders with stakes in the nonprofit sector, including government, and not just focus on the uses of charitable and philanthropic resources.

Sustainability and durability. The authors correctly describe the grantmaker commitment to organizational effectiveness as a long-term process, if it is to succeed. The focus therefore should be on the sustainability and durability of grantees and program and project implementers. The philanthropic sector must take the next step from promoting effectiveness to guaranteeing sustainability. Nonprofits are concerned with surviving over the time frames necessary to achieve the impacts they are looking for in systemic issues—welfare reform, community development, and civil rights, for example. A few funders, such as the Cowell Foundation and The Edna McConnell Clark Foundation, work with grantees to develop long-term sustainability plans for the organization, which are different from run-of-the-mill strategic plans, SWOT (strengths, weaknesses, opportunities, threats) analyses, or wish lists that dominate much of the field. However, for all the capacity-building and organizational effectiveness interventions in the field, few get down to the brass tacks of long-term financial planning with an eye toward the eventual, inevitable departure of charismatic nonprofit leaders and the turbulence that creates.

Defining effectiveness and capacity in turbulent communities in a turbulent world. As the authors acknowledge, there is still no hard-and-fast definition through the philanthropic world as to the parameters and indicators of nonprofit effectiveness. At a time when the social safety net built over the past several decades has been unraveled by both political parties, when for-profit commercial entities are encouraged to compete and sometimes given preferential treatment for the functions and resources that nonprofits frequently dominated on behalf of disadvantaged and disenfranchised populations, when threats to the advocacy and free speech rights of nonprofits crop up with increasing regularity, bolstering nonprofit effectiveness is no cakewalk. Nonprofit effectiveness extends beyond the boundaries of the organization to the intersection and interaction of the nonprofit sector and society. An operational definition of nonprofit effectiveness reflecting the turbulence and challenges of these times is something thoughtful grantmakers should earnestly seek.

Candor both ways. Candor is both feasible and desirable. For example, when The California Wellness Foundation ratcheted up its baseline commitment to operating support grants to roughly 50 percent of total grants, candor was an unexpected by-product. No longer forced to "pretzel" core operating support needs to fit project or program grant categories, the foundation's grant recipients opened up about the problems and challenges they were facing in surviving and functioning effectively. Candor is a great boon in the dynamic of foundations and nonprofits partnering for increased organizational effectiveness. It is also strikingly rare, not only in the interactions of nonprofits with their funders but sometimes even between nonprofits and their capacity builders. If operating support helps induce two-way candor, the majority of foundations still have not absorbed the lesson. For the top hundred foundations, grants specifically for nonprofit core operating costs dropped from 16.1 percent of total grant dollars in 1994 to 7.1 percent in 2000, rising only to 11 percent in 2001. If those top hundred foundations had made operating support grants in 2000 at a rate comparable to the next nine hundred foundations (18.3 percent), that would have amounted to $1 billion in additional core operating support. Based on the California Wellness example, that might have sparked some significantly increased candor.

Nonetheless, many nonprofits have deep-seated misgivings about the capacity of foundations to address the issue of nonprofit effectiveness. Even nonprofits known for raking in the grant dollars grumble and complain about their foundation partners, suggesting that the vast majority of this nation's sixty-four thousand foundations have a long way to go in addressing their own effectiveness, building their own capacities, and making their own board more responsible and productive before addressing the problems of nonprofit organizations.

Most nonprofits tell the unvarnished truth only to one another. Even the nation's toughest nonprofit advocates seem to choke on frogs when given the opportunity to say what's really on their mind about foundations to their foundations. They fear, sometimes with good reason, that critical feedback will be rewarded with grant rejections. The result is a stalemate: they have criticisms and misgivings about elements of foundations' organizational effectiveness agendas and strategies, but they fail to convey those concerns with vigor and honesty to their foundation funders. One of the delightful aspects of a volume such as *Funding Effectiveness* is that the authors represent the best of funder program staff, hungry for honest feedback, eager to learn from their grantees and make changes in their grantmaking initiatives and grossly disappointed when the nonprofits fail to give them the critical feedback they need. Nonprofits cannot grouse about the pace of funder attention to nonprofit effectiveness or the quality of some foundation-funded initiatives if they cannot find the courage to make their concerns clear to their funders.

In several different ways, the authors describe productive efforts in building nonprofit effectiveness as requiring an alignment between organizational values, mission, and program, applicable to both the funders and the nonprofits themselves. For the nonprofits, the critical element needed is candor, the willingness to tell the funders what they need, to tell the funders when they are getting bunk and pabulum under the rubric of organizational effectiveness work, and what they are willing to do to make the process better. The entire nonprofit sector's effectiveness would be enhanced by a massive dose of forthright dialogue. As Mark Twain noted, "When in doubt, tell the truth. It will confound your enemies and astound your friends." Straightforward nonprofit feedback on what works and what flops in the foundation efforts to build more effective nonprofits might reveal lots of astonished and truly appreciative funder allies.

References

Forbes, D. P. "Measuring the Unmeasurable: Empirical Studies of Nonprofit Organization Effectiveness from 1977 to 1997." *Nonprofit and Voluntary Sector Quarterly*, 1998, *27*(2), 183–202.

The Foundation Center. *Foundation Giving Trends: Update on Funding Priorities*. New York: The Foundation Center, 2003.

Herman, R. D., and Renz, D. O. "Theses on Nonprofit Organizational Effectiveness." *Nonprofit and Voluntary Sector Quarterly*, 1999.

Letts, C. W., Ryan, W. P., and Grossman, A. "Virtuous Capital: What Foundations Can Learn from Venture Capitalists." *Harvard Business Review*, Mar.-Apr. 1997, pp. 2–7.

Letts, C. W., Ryan, W. P., and Grossman, A. *High-Performance Nonprofit Organizations: Managing Upstream for Greater Impact*. New York: Wiley, 1999.

Light, P. C. *Pathways to Nonprofit Excellence*. Washington, D.C.: Brookings Institution Press, 2002.

Payton, R. *Philanthropy: Voluntary Action for the Public Good*. New York: Macmillan, 1988.

Stevens, S. K. "Tomorrow's Nonprofit: 7 Strategies for Managing Your Financial Future." *Nonprofit Times*, 1999, *13*(3), 41–43.

Sullivan, K. "Performance Measurement in Nonprofit Organizations: An Exploratory Case Study in Three Stages of the 1992–93 Pilot Self-Assessment Process of the Nonprofit Child Welfare Agencies Delivering Foster Care Services Under Contract with New York City's Child Welfare Administration." Doctoral dissertation, New York University, 1995. UMI Dissertation Services.

Index